Worth Keeping:

Life with My Extraordinary Daughter

Jean O'Malley Sigler
With
Elizabeth Sigler

To Marge, who showed me I can survive anything

Contents

Acknowledgements

I will always be grateful to the people who came into Liz's life and decided to stay on. My story would be very different and not nearly as beautiful if it weren't for all of you. I couldn't begin to name you all individually, but you know who you are. Thank you and I love you.

A huge thanks goes to my dedicated, hard-working editors and proofreaders, Duffy, Denny, Bob, Denise, Andy, Barb and Molly. I couldn't have done this without your sharp eyes and wicked sharp minds.

And above all, to Bob, David and Andy. You have loved her well.

Author's Note:

Some chapters include comments written by Liz. These comments are prefaced by the phrase, "In Liz's Words . . ."

While they are sometimes difficult to follow, I have not edited the comments as they are meant to give the reader a glimpse into the way Liz's mind works.

Dear Liz,

Well, I finally finished the book. I don't remember if I told you why I decided to write a book about you. The reason is that all your life, when I would tell people something remarkable or comical you had said or done, they would say, "I hope you are writing these things down," or "You need to write a book about Liz!" So I decided I had better do it, or all of those people would think I was lazy. The more I wrote, the more I was reminded of how many interesting and funny things you have said and done. Because of you, my life has often been fascinating and funny and every once in a very great while a little bit like hitting myself over the head with a hammer. That's okay, though, because if it weren't for you and our ups and downs, my time on this earth would probably have been awfully dull.

I called the book Worth Keeping because of a thank-you note you sent to Robin before she died. I told you that, besides saying thank you, you should say something about the gift. You wrote, "Thank you for the billfold, it is worth keeping." Every time I think about that note it makes me smile. I thought it would be wonderful to have a book lying on the table that makes me smile every time I see it.

Thank you for your contributions to the book. I think the things you have written will help people understand a little bit about what it is like to be you and that you are Liz Sigler first and a person with a disability second.

I admire so many things about you. You never stop trying to understand things even if they are confusing. You try to keep informed about what is going on in the world by reading the paper. Whatever job you have, you do it well. I have never seen or heard you make fun of anyone. You try hard to use appropriate social behavior. You are a faithful friend. You don't feel sorry for yourself. You are kind. As a friend of ours put it, you are a special soul.

I am so proud of the wonderful woman you have become. You should be proud, too. I feel lucky to be your mother. It has been my special privilege and I wouldn't exchange you for any daughter in the world!

I Love You,

Mom

p.s. There is not much in this book about Dad, David and Andy. That is not because they haven't been very important and helpful in your life, or because they don't love you just as much as I do. It is because the only story I can tell truthfully is my own, which is the only one I really know. Your dad and brothers each has his own story, just as you have yours. I am so proud of all of you!

Sigler Syndrome

When the nurse put Elizabeth in my arms a moment after she was born, she lay still and quiet. Unlike her brothers who fussed and wriggled, their faces all screwed up and squinchy, she seemed to look right into my eyes as if she recognized me from somewhere. I think now maybe she did. I held her gaze and whispered, "You can be anything you want to be."

The women's movement was well under way by then and I was thrilled to have a daughter I could guide through a life that held infinite possibilities. I imagined sitting proudly behind the podium on her inauguration day or snapping photos at her graduation from an Ivy League university. Maybe she would thank me from the stage as she accepted her Emmy or credit me for instilling in her the passion for world peace that eventually landed her the Nobel Prize. My fantasies were reinforced when I learned a couple of days later that Lizzie had been born with a caul. I read that that meant she was a child of the stars, destined for greatness. The possibilities danced in my head like sugar plums

I knew that her name would be shortened from Elizabeth. I vowed that the nickname would be Liz – classy and corporate – never Lizzie.

When I look at the newborn photographs now, I can see that, like most of her roomies in the nursery, Elizabeth was red and puffy and wrinkly – not at all the way I remember. Truth be told, she looked a lot like Winston Churchill.

My husband Bob and I brought Elizabeth home from the hospital and watched, completely enthralled, as she slept in her bassinet. Her brothers' reactions were pretty typical for their ages. David made goo-goo eyes at her for the first day and then went about the important business of a seven-year old. Andy, just three, failed to understand what he was supposed to be excited about when all she meant to him was theft of my attention, lots of disgusting bodily fluids running out all over the place, and house arrest.

As I fed my baby girl, I fantasized about what it would be like to have a daughter who would do girl things with me. Shopping with her brothers was like going on a 50 mile forced march, but Liz and I would have lots of trips to the mall, trying on clothes and funny hats, stopping for lunch, and maybe getting a mani\pedi. Even though I'm not much for baking, I imagined she would like it and would tease and cajole until we spent all of our Saturdays making cookies and cupcakes and talking about boyfriends and make-up.

We would snuggle in bed on winter week-ends watching chick-flick marathons while she shared her secret dreams with me. I knew she would be athletic, even though neither her parents nor brothers were. I was already organizing pre-meet dinners and caravans to out-of-town games. Eventually, I would have to control the number of sleepovers. She would be exhausted if she accepted all the invitations.

All suitors would be screened by her dad and me before she set foot out the door, not a day before her sixteenth birthday and only on double dates until she was 18. I pictured the dress she would wear to her first dance. It would be feminine, modest, and understated. She would be absolutely forbidden to show anything like cleavage until she was well into her second year of marriage. And of course, she wouldn't dream of wearing jeans or tank tops to a party no matter what the trending fashion. My girl would have class and taste. She would always seek my fashion advice and we would agree on every outfit she wore.

She would have a hard time deciding among all the universities that would court her, but with my guidance, she would pick the one that had the most to offer this remarkable young woman.

For her wedding, no more than four bridesmaids. Any more would be ostentatious. The color choices would be up to her, of course, but I was pretty sure she would agree that periwinkle blue dresses with bouquets of tiny red roses is a hard combination to beat. Her dress would be of buttery soft silk, absolutely no tulle!

When I think back I see that I might have been a tiny bit over the top on some of this. Donna Reed would have been jealous of the life I'd conjured for us, but a mother can dream, can't she?

Lizzie (my nickname resolve didn't last long) did nothing to cause me to alter my dreams. She was a practically perfect baby. She never cried -- really. Her "aunt" Martha said she only cried twice and once was when the doctor swatted her on the bottom when she was born. She kept to a textbook schedule from the first, slept through the night at two months, and stayed in bed until we went in to get her in the morning. I was in heaven.

Even as an older baby she didn't seem to need much attention. Most of the time she entertained herself. The littlest thing would hold her interest for a long time – a musical mobile, the TV, a soda can that she could roll, or a piece of cellophane she could crunch in her hand. She would ride in the car or the stroller or the grocery cart for long stretches without objecting.

There were only a couple of things that seemed to bother her. One was being handled too much. When I changed her clothes or diaper, she howled and hurled herself around as if she were trying to escape hellfire. I figured out that I should never to try to dress or change her unless I gave her a bottle at the same time. Then she sipped happily as if I didn't exist. And while this peculiarity pretty much ruled out playing dress-up with my new little doll, it was of minor importance. It did pose a problem one night when we went out. The babysitter was a friend's daughter. I left her with all the instructions for feeding and bedtime, but I forgot to tell her about the bottle trick. Her mom phoned me the next day to say that her daughter had called in a panic because Lizzie was shrieking and writhing so violently the girl couldn't get her sleeper on. They only lived a block away, so the sitter's mom came down and together they wrestled Lizzie into her jammies. They were both completely flummoxed because, as my friend said, "Lizzie never cries."

The only other thing that upset Lizzie was when people got right up in her face and tried to make her laugh with silly noises or goofy expressions. It seemed to make her uneasy. She would look away and become agitated and fussy.

At her six-month check-up, the pediatrician asked if I had any concerns. I told him that other than the dressing thing and the up-close contact, not much seemed to faze her. She never caused a fuss: she went to bed without a fuss; if she missed her nap she pushed through without a fuss; when I left her with other people she didn't fuss. She didn't even fuss when I told her everyone in the family was a Cubs fan. "She seems too good," I said. He looked at me like I had two heads to be complaining about a good baby and told me I was lucky. I was definitely not complaining, but Lizzie seemed remarkably good, so I remarked on it. Sometimes I think doctors only want you to remark on the things they understand. I didn't want to borrow trouble, though, so if the doctor said she was fine, I was fine. Besides, she babbled and cooed and smiled and sat up when other babies did.

Time marched on and before I knew it, Lizzie was a year old. It bothered me a little that she still wasn't walking. She didn't crawl either. She dragged herself around by her elbows, sort of like a wounded soldier making his way under the barbed wire to get back to his unit. Everyone assured me there was nothing to worry about. "None of my kids crawled." "Her cousin didn't walk until he was over a year old." "Lots of children who walk late are extra bright and graduate from Harvard." "Nobody ever crawled down the aisle to get married." Sometimes these remarks were reassuring, but sometimes what I saw outweighed the reassurance.

When Lizzie was 16 months old, we were at my mother's house on Easter Sunday. Lizzie sat in the middle of the back yard while her brothers and cousins tore around trying to find the most chocolate bunnies and eggs. I had hoped the lure of the kids scrambling about or the candy scattered across the lawn would inspire Lizzie to walk. In fact, she didn't seem interested in the egg hunt or her cousins. She sat in her own little world, oblivious to the festivities going on around her, happily eating her candy. I have a photograph of Lizzie in her Easter bonnet, sitting all alone in the grass that Easter Sunday. Whenever I look at it, I am back in that sunny yard, wishing the excited shouts of the other children could drown out the voice in my head that said something was just not right.

The next day I decided that I should get Lizzie checked out and at least make sure there was no medical reason why she was not walking. The first stop was the orthopedic doctor. Since I had already had two pediatricians tell me that despite her non-ambulatory approach to the world, Lizzie looked okay to them, I thought maybe a different specialty would look at her in a different way and possibly shed some light on what was going on. The doctor came into the examining room and asked me some questions. Then he asked me to take Lizzie's diaper off so he could check out her legs and hips and other walking parts. I did, and as soon as the cool air hit, she peed on the examining table. Mortified, I swiped my shirt sleeve over the puddle in the hope that the doctor hadn't noticed. He reached for a paper towel but realized that I had made it unnecessary. It suddenly occurred to me what I had done, but I was too embarrassed to be disgusted that my sleeve now reeked of baby urine. The doctor manipulated Lizzie's knees and hips and put her down on the floor to see how she crawled. She pooped on the carpet. I started toward her, but he grabbed a piece of the tissue that covered the exam table, picked up the offending lump, and threw it in the trash. He looked alarmed, but not about Lizzie. I think he was worried that I would gather up the dropping in my hands and put it in my purse. And I might have. When you are waiting for what could possibly be a life sentence, a little turd in the pocketbook doesn't seem like that big a deal.

Having moved through the pooptastrophe, the doctor had Lizzie walk holding on to his fingers. He said, "Well, I'm not sure what is going on but we should run some tests. It could be cerebral palsy. Or with the way she walks on her toes, it could be some kind of degenerative brain condition." Now wait just a minute here! How did we get from a little delay in walking to disastrous, lifelong illness in 15 minutes and a couple of potty accidents? I told him that toe walking was a long and honored tradition in my husband's family. Her dad and both of her Sigler uncles, several nieces and nephews and one of her brothers are all happily gamboling through life like dancers en pointe and they don't have degenerative brain conditions. I also mentioned that Liz's paternal genes carried quite a bit of klutz down through the generations. Her dad never undertook a job involving manual labor that didn't end in bleeding and band aids. By the time he was six, David had been to the emergency room for stitches so often that the last time we took him in, a social worker came to talk to us about the frustrations of parenting. Bless her heart, she thought we were flinging the poor kid down the stairs or pushing him off the swing set on purpose. We must have answered the questions the right way, because they let us leave with David, although I almost threw a coat over his poor, stitched head just in case they were looking to put him in the system. I'll never forget a day when Andy called out to me to watch him turn the soil for my garden. I looked over just in time to see him drive the pitchfork through his shoe, almost severing a toe. Just another day at Camp Swampy for us.

I suggested that the doctor check with a lifelong friend of Lizzie's dad, who was also a doctor, for confirmation of all I had reported. He left the room for a short time, returned and said, "Okay, I talked to Dr. Jim and he convinced me that it is probably not CP or a brain condition. I still think it is a syndrome of some kind, but for now I'll call it Sigler Syndrome." It occurs to me that I never recounted this story to my husband's family. I think they will be mighty proud to know they might someday end up in an AMA journal article.

Not wanting to set us and our syndrome loose on the world without at least trying to fix something, the doctor noted that Lizzie not only walked on her toes, but that they pointed out. He allowed as how even that was unusual because it is typically boys who toe out while girls tend to be pigeon toed. This gave me a whole new set of things to worry about as David toed in on the left foot and out on the right. I didn't know whether I should worry more about his orthopedic status or his gender confusion. I put this latest maternal anxiety on a back burner and took the prescription for a "Dennis Brown" splint to the pharmacy. I was given a pair of shoes attached to a steel rod that Lizzie was to wear to bed every night in an effort to get her toes to go in a girl direction. That night, typical of her, when I laced her little feet into the Denny Brown, she didn't seem to notice that her legs were spread apart and her feet turned at an angle that would make sleep impossible even for a pigeon. But not for Lizzie. She went directly to sleep that night and every night thereafter while she wore the thing. I can't remember when or why we stopped using it, but it didn't change the way she walked, so the "Denny" departed our lives. For the record, David still toes in on one side and out on the other, but he seems comfortable with both his gait and his sexual identity.

The last thing the orthopedic doctor had done before we left was to recommend that Lizzie be seen by a neurologist. He really wasn't going to let us go gently. This made me uneasy. If an orthopedic doctor was concerned about a neurological condition, I was too. I made an appointment as soon as I got home.

The neurologist played with Lizzie and did those secret evaluations that neurologists can do when you think they are just visiting with you, but they are really detecting a large and invasive brain tumor just by the way you smile. He picked her up and bounced her on his knee and said, "She looks just fine to me. If you don't want her, my wife will take her." When I heard this, I wanted to jump across the desk and chew the guy's face off. If I didn't want her indeed! I was referred to him by one of his colleagues who didn't like what he saw. I was terrified there was something seriously wrong with my baby, and now I had to listen to flip, toss-off remarks? I left the doctor's office flustered by his arrogance but relieved at his conclusion. Lizzie was fine – I was crazy – a diagnosis that would be made often in the years to come. As it turns out this doctor came back into our lives later on when Lizzie began having seizures. She still sees him and I have completely revamped my opinion of him. He is my favorite of all the doctors Lizzie has seen. That could be due to the fact that he is a good and kind man, though it might have something to do with the fact that he is a knee-jerk liberal and likes to talk baseball.

Lizzie finally walked at 17 months – late, but not off-the - charts late. The pediatrician informed me that seventeen months wasn't really even considered "delayed." I wondered if he noticed that she walked like a drunken sailor, staggering and waving her arms, but I kept still. I was beginning to doubt whether I really wanted the doctors' opinions. I seemed to disagree with them whichever way they went. Besides, I was so relieved that Lizzie would toddle her way through the last few months of toddlerhood that I didn't want to borrow trouble.

Exiting the Donna Reed Highway

Although Lizzie's navigational skills eventually caught up to those of her peers, her language was much slower to develop. Slow isn't exactly the right word. She said words and formed sentences on time, but she didn't communicate her feelings or needs like her brothers had. She seemed confused by what people said to her, partly because she interpreted most of what was said in a completely literal way. That idiosyncrasy gave rise to some funny stuff.

At two and a half she could say the alphabet backwards, and whenever we asked her to perform her trick, she turned around and recited the letters from *Z* to *A* while she walked in reverse. I did love that one. A few years ago my friend broke her ankle and was in a cast for a while. She could only navigate the stairs if she hopped up facing the wrong way round. She told me that whenever she went to the second floor, she had the urge to say the alphabet backwards.

When she was three, I asked Lizzie, who was looking quite green around the gills, if she felt like she was going to throw up. I have a "throw up" bowl reserved for just such occasions, so when she nodded, I gave it to her. She threw the bowl up into the air and tossed her cookies on the kitchen floor.

Just before she turned four she had an exam to determine if she had a lazy eye. The ophthalmologist said, "Okay Lizzie, now I want you to look right into the light." As he started to swing his chair around to shine his penlight in her eyes, Lizzie stood up in the chair, turned around and looked directly into the light that was attached to the back wall. It was the one that illuminated the E chart. The doctor looked perplexed for a minute and then smiled sheepishly and apologized for not explaining properly.

As a preschooler, Lizzie did other unique and mysterious things.

At the lazy-eye exam the nurse put a chart on the wall and, pointing to a picture of an elephant, asked Lizzie to name the animal. When Lizzie didn't respond, I told her that Lizzie would do better with the letter chart. The nurse, looking puzzled, said they didn't use the letter chart on children Lizzie's age because either they didn't know their letters or they weren't consistent in identifying them. When I explained that Lizzie wasn't consistent in her identification of pictures, but never missed on letters, the nurse switched to the letter chart and Lizzie didn't miss a single one until she covered her left eye. The doctor determined that Lizzie was an alphabet prodigy with strabismus. I think that, while correctly naming all the letters seemed a precocious thing for a four-year-old to do, it was easier for Lizzie because, while printed letters don't change, there are hundreds of ways to portray a shoe or a squirrel. Processing that kind of inconsistent information is still hard for her.

Another time, as I was reading to her, I asked her what she thought about something in the story. I hoped she would say she was scared or that something was funny to her – anything to indicate she understood what I was reading. Instead, she said, "Fifteen is yellow, too." I had no idea what she meant until she turned back to page 15. The page number, in dark black type, stood out from a bright yellow background – just like the page we were on – page 26. I was disappointed, but also fascinated by her uncommon perspective on things.

When the other children watched cartoons or Sesame Street, she wasn't interested and went off by herself. But when we left "To Kill a Mockingbird" in the VCR one summer, she watched it 20 times.

Lizzie continued to be an exceptionally agreeable child unless someone tried to get her to do something outside of her comfort zone. When that happened the devil himself was no match for her fury or persistence. She became enraged every time. Her routine was an absolute imperative for her, and pity the fool who thought she could be cajoled into stepping outside it.

In some cases that fool would be me. Take for instance the day I rearranged her bedroom while she was at her grandmother's house. All girls like a change once in a while, right? Oh how very wrong that is in Lizzie's case. She was so infuriated that I had to put everything back exactly where it was before she would go to bed that night. To this day she wants nothing disturbed in her room, and it is not out of some sense of order. I don't know how she gets from the door to the bed through the sea of brochures, shoes, stacks of coins, notes to herself, bowling equipment and bank statements. What I didn't see for a long time was that within the chaos, everything is always in the same place. In the 27 years we have lived in this house, I don't think anything in her room has been moved, except when she cleans, after which she replaces everything in the exact same spot, even the empty bins, baskets and tubs I have continued to buy to help her get organized. She has never wanted a desk with drawers or shelves or a closet in her room. Living in a 90-year old house that has one closet for every five rooms, she couldn't have a closet of her own even if she wanted it. She says it is hard for her to remember where things are if they are in drawers or behind closed doors.

Lizzie's behavior was at once bizarre and fascinating. She didn't play like the other little girls her age. She had lots of dolls, a Raggedy Ann doll, a baby doll, a Cabbage Patch doll, crocheted dolls and ceramic dolls, all of which remained on shelves decorating her bedroom. She never really played with them. She didn't have a Barbie doll because Democrats don't buy their daughters Barbie dolls. My one Republican friend's daughters had at least 71 Barbie dolls, the Barbie convertible, the Barbie Dream House, many other Barbie accoutrements and one exhausted looking Ken. They also had the Barbie hairdresser head. Instead of dressing and redressing the little pointy breasted Barbies in their stilettos and bustiers or changing Barbie's hairdo, Lizzie put the disembodied Barbie head in a stroller and pushed it around and around in a circle until I made her stop because I was afraid one of us was going to throw up.

She didn't seem to fear any of the things that had terrified her older brothers -- monsters, the dark, stray dogs posed no threat to Lizzie. Even potential abandonment didn't get her attention. Once, as I was checking out at the grocery store, I noticed that Lizzie wasn't beside me. I glanced back and saw she was in the freezer aisle. As I watched, she went up one side of the aisle then down the other methodically opening and closing each and every door. When she got to the end of the second aisle, she crossed over and began again. The aisle was long and Lizzie was tiny, so she seemed to get smaller and smaller the further down the aisle she went. When I called to her and told her it was time to go, she ignored me. I thought she was pretending not to hear the way children do when they don't want to stop an activity. I stopped calling to her for a minute and just watched as she continued on her never-ending mission. Looking back, that day seems like a metaphor for our life together. For years it seemed that, no matter how I called out to her, Liz drifted further and further away.

Trying to avoid a noisy contest of wills, I tried the age old ploy, "Okay then, I'm just going to go home and you can stay here." I got all the way to the door and Lizzie didn't bat an eye. Out of options, I swept her up and carried her, kicking and screaming, to the car. The thought of spending the rest of her life as a motherless child living in a supermarket did not seem to bother her. What bothered Lizzie was having to stop opening and closing those doors.

On the other hand, she was afraid of things that took me completely off guard. When she and her friend, Suzy, took swimming lessons together, Suzy, along with some of the other little tadpoles, was terrified of the water. Lizzie was unfazed by the prospect of sinking into the depths and was also indifferent to the stern, unsmiling teacher, who scared the crap out of me. What did scare her was the noise of the hair dryer in her ears. Unfortunately, these lessons took place in the middle of a Nebraska winter, so I felt duty bound to dry her hair at least a little before we ventured outside. Just about the time the other swimmers' panicked screams were subsiding, Lizzie was barely getting cranked up. After a couple of hair drying attempts that ended in blood-curdling shrieks, I jammed a thick stocking cap over her wet hair and made a beeline for the car. I was afraid the mean teacher lady would call the authorities, but I preferred getting arrested for transporting a frozen minor to enduring the wrath of Lizzie. She survived the lessons and the cold and learned how to swim somewhere along the line, but I don't think it was from that wicked witch of the water. I'll never know because she wouldn't let mothers stay to watch the lessons. She was really mean!

Every Christmas, the whole family gathered at my parents' house to celebrate and exchange gifts. The year Lizzie was six, my dad got my mother a brand new Polaroid camera. As we all descended to the basement to begin the frenzy of gift opening, my mother loaded her new toy with film. She arranged us accordingly and took the first photo. Some of us, including Liz, gathered round to watch the picture develop. Suddenly, Liz ran up the basement stairs. Puzzled, I followed her and found her at the front door. She said she wanted to go home. I tried to figure out what was scaring her so much that she was willing to forego all the Christmas loot, but I could get nothing from her. My mother came upstairs carrying her camera. Lizzie looked at it and repeated her urgent wish to leave. Putting two and two together, I asked her if she was afraid of the camera and she said she was not, but her eyes told a different story. This was to become a pattern with Lizzie. If there was any question in her mind that her response to something was different from other people, she denied it. Over the years I have become quite the detective as I try to interpret what she is feeling. In the Case of the Petrifying Polaroid, I think seeing the images of herself and other family members, slowly emerging through the developing solution like denizens of the deep, was very disconcerting to Liz. I have to say, it creeps me out too. Only after Nana put the Polaroid on the high shelf of a closet and vowed that it would remain there forevermore did Lizzie agree to rejoin the festivities.

Potty training was tricky. Lizzie was already three and I couldn't decide how to approach the issue. Her language problem stood in the way. I couldn't entice her with big girl panties, because she just didn't get it. Also it was hard to explain to someone who has trouble processing anything abstract why it was time to completely change the way she had done something all her life, with the only upside being a newfound dignity. After reading a couple of articles on the subject, I decided to try something unconventional. I got a bag of potato chips and a liter of soda pop and planted Lizzie on the potty chair in front of the TV to watch game shows. She would have watched "The Price is Right" and "Wheel of Fortune" until the sun set if they had been in syndication back then. By that time she was already reading some words and knew her numbers. I owe Vanna White a big thanks for the reading. Bob Barker and "Come on Down!" get the credit for teaching Lizzie numbers. Anyway, after a full morning of drinking and viewing, Lizzie's bladder couldn't hold the pop, and she let loose in the potty chair. I said, "Good job," put her in training pants and she never wore a diaper again. The more serious part of the bathroom experience was just as easy, except that she would absolutely not move her little bowels unless she was holding onto a book. I think she read Freud before she was born. I was beginning to see that my girl would probably always have her own way of doing things, and it probably wouldn't be my way, but once she learned something, she never forgot it.

I wanted Lizzie to go to preschool like all the other kids, but I couldn't imagine her being able to do the same kinds of activities as other four-year olds in a preschool setting. She could recognize all the letters and numbers, but had trouble with the simplest drawing task. Her coloring was all over the page. She couldn't sing the words to the children's songs or tell what had happened in a story. I knew she would not be able to follow the directions given by the teacher or understand the social rules of the preschooler.

I heard about a church preschool that emphasized language development. I went to the school and talked to the teacher and she thought it might be a good place for Lizzie. She started there the next week; just before she turned four. Things went well for the first couple of months. At least Lizzie didn't object to going and no one told me about any problems until parent conferences in the late fall. The teacher told me she was concerned about Lizzie's progress. She told me Lizzie couldn't work puzzles like the other kids; she couldn't follow directions like the other kids; she couldn't draw simple shapes like the other kids; she didn't play with the other kids. The teacher recommended that I have Lizzie tested by the public school Early Intervention program.

When an experienced teacher compares your child to a classroom full of her peers and your child comes up short in most of the comparisons, it is not good. When that teacher recommends evaluation by the special education department of the school system, it is really not good. All of the fears and suspicions that had been hovering around the back of my mind for three years came racing to the front. I had been trying to believe family, friends and doctors, but I knew in my heart that there was something going on in her brain that made Lizzie different from other children.

I called the number the teacher gave me and made an appointment with what was to be the first of many specialists and professionals who would become part of our lives. Lizzie and I were about to exit the Donna Reed highway.

Where's Annie Sullivan
When You Need Her?

Lizzie and I came together with the psychologists in a stuffy, windowless room. We sat in small, kid-sized chairs around a rectangular table. Or maybe the chairs weren't small. Maybe I just felt small sitting opposite these women who were about to re-write the script of my life. I can't be sure. One of the women sat with her pen poised above her writing pad. I hoped against hope that she was writing "child fine-mother overreacting," but I realized she was recording her observations of Lizzie and my interactions with her. In my mind, she was making the definitive evaluation of me as a mother. I concentrated on making sure I did everything right so she didn't put in her notes that whatever was wrong with my daughter was probably my fault.

The other woman began to explain the results of the IQ exam. She said that Lizzie's performance level was below what would be expected of a child her age. When she told me that Lizzie had missed an item on the test because she didn't know how to draw a straight line when directed, I jumped on the chance to show these people how wrong they were. I asked for permission to demonstrate that Lizzie should definitely get a pass on this question. I told her to go to the black board and draw a "one." She did it on the spot. See? That's a more sophisticated task than drawing a straight line, right? Any old four-year old can make a mark, but my four-year old knows how to write a number. I waited for the woman's "aha" moment to happen, but she said that it would still be marked as a failed item.

The psychologists continued by saying they had found Lizzie to be developmentally delayed. Well now, that wasn't so bad. I would just have to work with her more until she caught up. I asked the woman when she thought that might happen. She said that in this case, "delayed" meant something different. Lizzie's test scores indicated that she would not be catching up. I should have said, "Then why use a word that holds out a handful of hope just to snatch it back when the mother reaches for it?" I didn't think of that until much later, though. I was having a hard time thinking at all.

I asked the woman the specific IQ results for Lizzie's tests, but she hesitated to reveal the number. I cajoled her into telling by hauling out my special education credentials, recounting my 11 years of experience teaching in special education classrooms. Reluctantly she said, "Sixty-nine, but I think it is higher." I thought I remembered that an IQ of 69 falls into the "Trainable Mentally Handicapped" range, the terminology used in 1982. The woman continued to talk and interpret other test results, but I didn't really hear her. She was saying a lot, but little was actually getting through to me. As she reeled off lists of tests and results, all of the terms, past and present that had been used to describe people with developmental disabilities came to my mind. "Retarded," "Imbecile," "Idiot," "Moron," "Subnormal," "Mentally Handicapped." The words crashed into each other and exploded into a thousand pieces inside my head. It was all I could do to remain in that room until the women were finished with us. I just wanted to run -- out and away.

Lizzie's dad, an attorney, was in court and couldn't be reached, so as soon as I got home I called my mother. She rushed over to my house and held me while I sobbed my fears for my baby girl's future. Would she ever understand anything she read? Would she have friends? Would she go to the prom? Would she get a job? Would she be able to live alone when Bob and I were no longer here? My mother tried to comfort me. She told me later that it was one of the hardest days of her life. Now that I am a grandmother, I know how heartbreaking it was for her. She not only had to hear this news about her precious grandbaby, she had to stand by helpless in the face of her own child's anguish. From that moment on, until she died, when Lizzie was 23, my mother was one of her primary teachers. In fact, Lizzie has always credited her grandmother with most of her accomplishments. She still says that Nana taught her most of the words she ever learned when they played Scrabble during overnight visits. Nana taught her how to play hearts and gin rummy and gave her manicures and taught her table manners. I was nothing more than the transportation that got her to this fountain of knowledge, wisdom and caring that she couldn't find at home. I'm pretty sure Liz believes that, if it weren't for Nana, she would have languished in my care with chipped nails and ragged cuticles, unable to speak coherently, eating peas off a knife.

I had somehow thought that I would feel better if I had a diagnosis – something to hang my hat on, something that would point the way for intervention and cures and such. Instead I alternated between feeling devastated and numb. I walked around wondering when someone was going to take charge of this situation, because it didn't look like I was going to step up to the plate any time soon. Grappling with the idea that there was indeed something wrong with my baby took up all my mental energy those first weeks.

I did enroll Lizzie in a special education preschool beginning the following Monday as the Early Intervention staff had advised. They said the sooner we intervened the better it would be for Lizzie. So, while her little friends were going to preschool for three half-days a week, I handed my little girl over to a special education van driver who would take her across town to a "Handicapped Preschool" where she would go all day every day.

I sat in the empty house on Lizzie's first day of school trying to figure out what I should be doing. I felt the pressure of being a special education teacher. I knew the world would be watching and waiting to see how I snatched this child from the jaws of mental retardation by hard work and sheer force of will. I didn't have the energy at that point to create the seminal early intervention program, but I thought I could at least write about the experience of having a child with a disability, so I began a journal. It started something like, "Thus began our journey together" or "Now our work would begin." I didn't get past the first page, because I realized immediately that I was setting myself up. I would have to be insightful and inspiring and make the journal a record of how I never gave up until Lizzie exceeded any expectations held for a little mentally handicapped girl. I was afraid people would expect the two of us to perform like Helen Keller and Annie Sullivan. The world would be holding its breath waiting for me to produce a sea change both in my daughter and in all early childhood special education.

Not only did I have Annie Sullivan peering over my shoulder, I had my mother, figuratively speaking. My mother, Marge, actually did rescue my brother from a life spent in a wheelchair. Duffy got polio when he was seven years old. After six months in the hospital and countless hours of physical therapy, the doctors told Marge that my brother would never stand again, but that they would continue with therapy for a while longer, anyway. My mother said that since the professionals didn't seem to be able to do any more to help her son, she would just go ahead and take him on home.

As soon as she got Duffy settled, Marge set up a neighborhood novena and a friends-and-family therapy schedule. She made a special wheelchair out of a dining room chair that was narrow enough to get through the doorways of our little house. She notified the public schools that her son would not be attending the special school for children who had polio. Instead, he would be going to his neighborhood Catholic school. Then she informed the principal of the parish school that my brother would not be attending school on icy days. Duffy would come to school only as long as he could walk into the building under his own steam.

So, in addition to defying all medical predictions by getting her son up and walking, my mother arranged for my brother to attend his neighborhood school 20 years before inclusion for kids with disabilities was even considered, much less mandated. Talk about a hard act to follow!

In the end, what I did was to get on with things. That's what we do in my family. Not that we're stoic. We're not afraid to let the world know that we are suffering, and we definitely want credit for the extraordinary effort we put forth. But once given the sympathy due us, we grab hold of the bootstraps and pull. That is not to say that I took all this in stride. Every time a professional told me about some other area where Lizzie came up short, my dreams for her crumbled all over again. Every time another child her age did something that Lizzie should have been doing but wasn't, my heart ached. Every time I saw the look of confusion in her eyes at some new mystery the world threw at her without explanation, I died a little. I wanted desperately to find the key to unlock these mysteries for her.

The "Handicapped" preschool was a good experience for Lizzie. The teacher was a speech language pathologist and there was an emphasis on language development all day, every day. The teacher and I agreed that language processing was at the core of Lizzie's difficulties. For some reason, her brain didn't make the same connections most of ours do, and she had a lot of trouble understanding what was said to her. She needed to learn the meaning of words and phrases almost one at a time. The teacher gave us an example of something that troubled her. Apparently, Lizzie didn't seem to know the difference between 'sink' and 'float'. I had not noticed this, maybe because we didn't talk that much about sinking and floating at our house. I tried to think of situations where this confusion could become a problem, but aside from actually experiencing the former when expecting the latter, I couldn't. I was more worried by the fact that some of the time Lizzie didn't seem to know the difference between her arse and her elbow, but I kept that to myself.

The teacher suggested that I should model correct language for Lizzie by talking to her a lot, explaining everything I did and every thought I had. Unfortunately, at home I mostly speak when spoken to and pare down any explanation about anything until there is only a core left that no one but me understands. I tried to chatter for a couple of days, but it exhausted me, so I went to the toy store and bought a battery operated contraption that called out phrases in a disturbing singsong computer voice. The listener was to find the picture card that matched the phrase and put it on a rack. The game was supposed to improve language development and comprehension skills. All it did was scare the bejesus out of Lizzie. I returned it and replaced it with a tape recorder and some story books on tape. Since she could already read, the exercise didn't really teach Lizzie anything, but she spent hours, days, and years listening to those books which more or less let me off the talking hook. I got lots of language workbooks and word games and worked on them with Lizzie almost daily.

Far from getting the praise I expected, I was called out by one of the Early Intervention professionals for working with Lizzie too much. She said, "It is obvious that someone has done a lot of work with your daughter, but does anyone play with her?" Well, here's the thing, I am not good at playing. My imagination for being the auntie while Lizzie was the mommy lasted about 10 minutes. I am convinced I don't have a right side to my brain. I like working puzzles, building blocks, organizing doll outfits, and putting together complicated toys. Once I have assembled the play kitchen, the play crib, the doll house or the stroller, I'm pretty much through with it. Lizzie is even less inclined than I to comfort a pretend baby or drive to the pretend grocery store to buy pretend bread and milk. So, I guess we didn't play enough. . . But there was an advantage to this. I cleared quite a nice profit a few years later when I sold her mint condition toys in a garage sale

My Short Life of Crime

At the year-end preschool conference Lizzie's teacher recommended that she go to an integrated kindergarten the following year. The new teacher would also be a speech language pathologist. Most of the children would have language disorders like Lizzie. The integration would be provided by neighborhood children who were in the class and had developmentally appropriate language.

The idea behind the integrated kindergarten was that typical children would mix it up with the language disordered kids and be language role models for them. Unfortunately, Lizzie's problems were too extensive to be cured by listening to other five-year olds stumble their way through idioms, semantics and grammar rules. She did, however, imitate her typical peers to some extent. Her particular classroom was located in an inner city school and many of the neighborhood kids were African-American. No problem there, but after a few months, when I told Lizzie it was time to go to bed, she responded, "What you talkin' bout, Girl?" It was a bit strange hearing Lizzie speaking Ebonics in her little white-bread world, and fortunately, that was the only time she did. A bigger issue turned out to be that she imitated her parents. One evening Bob and I were sitting at the kitchen table talking when Lizzie came tearing into the room, opened the towel drawer and said frantically, "I need a dammit!" She grabbed a towel, ran into the family room and began to wipe up the juice that had spilled. I could just hear her teachers saying, "When a child uses language like that, you know she is learning it in the home."

Lizzie had an uneventful year in Kindergarten. Well, except for the first day, and even that was uneventful for her. I had taken a picture of David then Andy as they headed off to the first day of Kindergarten, and I followed Lizzie outside to do the same on her big day. She looked cute as could be in her little skirt and blouse, but it wasn't the uniform of the Catholic school her brothers attended and she didn't walk to school with the neighborhood kids. She rode to school on a special education van. I snapped the photo, put her on the van, went inside and cried. It is strange the things that get to me the most, but it is still gut-wrenching to remember that day, even 20-some years later. Lizzie took the whole thing in stride. She wasn't fazed by the fact that she spent two hours each day being transported back and forth to a school five miles away. It would not be the last time I got my panties in a bunch over something that didn't bother her at all.

At the end of the term, it was time to figure out where she would spend her grade school years. That placement would be determined, in part, by her second psychological evaluation. After the first evaluation which qualifies a child to receive special education services, the school district conducts reevaluations every three years. Lizzie's second evaluation was in a different room with different people, but it took me right back to that first time when all I heard was "handicapped." I was gearing up for the school psychologist to corroborate the diagnosis of mental retardation that the Early Intervention team had made when Lizzie was four. My memory of this second meeting is crystal clear. The results of the evaluation were amazing. Lizzie scored 11 points higher on the IQ test and was now considered to be in the borderline/normal range of intelligence with a language disorder. I was ecstatic. My baby wasn't retarded after all! I was prepared to get t-shirts printed for her that said "Almost Normal." That designation put her miles ahead of millions of people in this life. I immediately called Bob and my mother and shared the fantastic test results. Ironically, this wonderful news plunged me into a crime spree unprecedented in the annals of special education evaluations.

My next call, after Bob and my mother, was to my friend, Linda. I had barely gotten a word out when she said breathlessly, "I just got back from the eye doctor and Heidi isn't going to go blind!" Her daughter had an eye disease which could have potentially caused blindness. "And Lizzie's not retarded!" I shouted gleefully. We decided we had to go out for a celebratory dinner that night.

I entered the restaurant and we grabbed each other and hugged and laughed and cried until the other customers began to look askance. We sat down over an adult beverage or two and shared every word the psychologists and eye doctor had said. Linda, never one to pass up a chance to throw a party, decided we had to mark this auspicious occasion in a special way. After much discussion we decided that the most dramatic thing we could do would be to dance in the fountain of a nearby upscale shopping center. I drove to the fountain, but we were bitterly disappointed to see that it had been shut down for the night. Linda wasn't giving up. "Get in the car. I have a better idea." She directed me to the "Old Mill," where a 30-foot high, brightly lit Dutch mill wheel advertised the strip mall. "Come on!" Linda ordered. I got out of the car and followed her like a puppy, wondering what in the hell she had in mind. She got to the edge of the mill pond and reached over to grab the wheel. As God is my witness, this nut job was going to step on one of the slats and ride the mill wheel to the top or to her death, whichever came first. At the precise moment Linda's hands touched the wheel, we heard the scream of a police siren as the cruiser came directly toward us, its flashing red lights nearly blinding us. The police car jumped the curb and rolled to a stop on the sidewalk next to us. I was horrified. Bob was a Deputy County Attorney at the time. These are the people who prosecute folks who were doing the kind of thing Linda was getting ready to do. All I could think of was the word "accessory" and not the stylin' kind. I tried to talk to Linda without moving my lips. "Whatever you do, don't tell this guy I'm Bob's wife!" "Well, of course I won't! Do you think I'm stupid?" she retorted. She stepped away from the mill wheel and cheerfully approached the patrol car calling, "Hi, Officer. Do you know Bob Sigler? This is his wife." I turned around and headed toward the mill pond with every intention of flinging myself in and peacefully drowning.

"Are you kidding me? You're Bob's wife?"

There followed about 45 minutes of wildly funny (to them) exchanges between Linda and the law enforcement officer. He mused about whether he should take me down for a breathalyzer, but since I hadn't been driving the millwheel when he got there, he didn't have much of a case. Linda asked him if the old saying was 'three hots *and* cot' or 'three hots *on* a cot.' He checked through his arrest book to see if there was a code for mill wheel riding on private property at 11:30 at night. He didn't find one that matched exactly, but he felt confident he would be able to figure something out. They tossed around ideas about what the headline should be if the newspaper got hold of this.

Finally, I could take no more. By then so much time had passed that my blood alcohol level had fallen dangerously low. 'Look Officer Krupke, I promise you I am okay to drive, but if you are just waiting for me to pull away so you can take me downtown, you'd best do it, because I'm really tired and I want to go home and go to bed so I'll be nice and fresh when all this becomes public tomorrow." He assured me he wasn't planning to arrest me. I got behind the wheel, put the car in gear, and pulled slowly away from the curb. The sirens resumed their screaming and the lights whirled around frantically. I looked over at him, furious at the betrayal. He was laughing so hard he could barely turn off the gizmos. I drove toward the street that I thought would get me back to the main drag and immediately got lost in the maze of stores and side streets. The officer took pity on me, pulled ahead and led me out of the shopping area. Since no arrest was made, my reputation as an upstanding citizen remained untarnished. Bob laughed harder than the cop.

Beyond kindergarten there weren't special classrooms for language disordered kids, so we had to decide what the best grade school placement for Lizzie would be. Because she received special education services, she had an Individualized Education

Plan (IEP). The IEP was developed by a team including the professionals who evaluated Lizzie, her teachers, and Bob and me. The plan enumerated specific goals, who would provide her special education services, and where they would be delivered. She was sent for two weeks to a Learning Disabilities (LD) evaluation center where they determined that she wouldn't fit in an LD classroom because, at five years of age, she could already read and the emphasis in these classrooms was on learning to read. Lizzie's teacher suggested that she might have Hyperlexia. That was a new term for me. I asked what it meant. She said it meant Lizzie read too much. How does that work? Kids spend a whole lot of their first few years of life being taught to read. When they finally master the skills, if they use them too much, they are accused of having the dreaded Hyperlexia? I guess this was also my fault. When I should have bought Lizzie a castle and played wicked witch to her fairy princess, I bought that damned tape recorder. I had created a kid who worked too much, read too much and didn't know sink from float. Her future looked pretty dim. When I did further reading on Hyperlexia, I learned that it was a little more complicated than that. Children with Hyperlexia are prodigious readers, but have great difficulty with comprehension. That was definitely true of Lizzie. Even though she could have read Webster's Third International Dictionary cover to cover at this point in her young life, she couldn't begin to explain why Jack and

Jill went up the hill. At any rate, a Learning Disabilities classroom was not an option.

Another possibility was a self-contained special education classroom in the neighborhood school where Lizzie would spend most, if not all, of the day. That didn't seem appropriate either. It seemed especially important that Lizzie be immersed in the language of typical kids. The IEP team decided that the best placement for Lizzie would be the regular first grade class. She would get extra help from a special education resource teacher and also speech\language services.

We identified a school with a particularly strong special education program and moved our family to a new house specifically so Lizzie could attend that school. Sadly, I chose a house right across the road from the houses where the children could attend the school with the strong special education program. The boundary ran right down the middle of our street. So now, in spite of my careful planning, Lizzie would be attending a school I knew absolutely nothing about. I was beginning to think I should just face up to my shortcomings, call social services, and turn Lizzie over to someone who could give her a fighting chance in this world; but I decided she would have to play the maternal hand that she had been dealt, so we enrolled her in the neighboring public school. Her brothers would continue at our parish school.

When fall came, Lizzie was transported to first grade, but this time she rode in my car instead of a van. We were making progress.

The Grade School Years

Lizzie did fairly well in first grade because she could already read and write her letters. Her math skills were above average for a first grader. She could master anything static like letters, numbers, and colors very quickly. Spelling was her strongest subject because words are, for the most part, spelled the same way every time. In fact, she was a spelling whiz. To this day Liz holds her elementary school's title for 1984 First Grade Spelling Bee Champion. But things that required analysis and interpretation, like stories or math thought problems were moving targets for her. She just did not understand them.

Many kind people suggested things we might try, like having Lizzie look up words in a dictionary and keeping a list of their meanings or having her do her studying by listening to tapes instead of reading from books. The more I tried to explain Lizzie's problem, the more I saw how complex it was. Using a dictionary wouldn't help her because the definition of a word was, to her, just more words she didn't understand. Auditory learning would be no better or worse than reading books for information because, in the end, comprehension requires that the words themselves be understood, whether read or heard. Context clues were useless. She didn't seem to have a future tense, so predicting what would happen in a story confounded her. It seemed as if she grasped the meaning of concepts one at a time, in isolation. It was labor intensive and, ultimately, an ineffective way to learn.

Another serious stumbling block to interpreting her surroundings was Lizzie's concrete view of the world. A great example of this was the "Hands Across America Day." Each person on our block paid a dollar to join hands in a human chain to raise awareness of hunger in this country. When I tried to explain to Lizzie that we had all given a dollar to stand at the side of a busy street holding hands so hungry people could eat, she said in all seriousness, "I'm hungry. Why doesn't anybody give me a dollar?"

One day at her school, an announcement came over the loudspeaker, asking everyone to pray for the principal who had lost his father the night before. Lizzie's response was less than prayerful, but, in her eyes, much more practical. "Why don't they just look for him?"

And speaking of abstract ideas . . . we enrolled Lizzie in religious education classes (CCD) at our parish so she could make her First Communion with the other first graders. While I was absolutely positive that she had no idea what the teacher was talking about, she went to class every week and took the whole thing in stride in her usual Lizzie fashion. A few days before the big event, her teacher called me and said that the religious education director didn't think Lizzie should receive her First Communion because she didn't understand transubstantiation. The main mystery of the Catholic faith, transubstantiation holds that during Mass, the Communion bread and wine are transformed into the body and blood of Jesus. I said to the CCD teacher, "Did you ask the director if *she* understands transubstantiation, because I sure don't and they punched my ticket!" The CCD teacher's day job was in special education and she was sympathetic. She agreed with me that we should let Lizzie put on her little white dress and veil and walk up to the Communion rail with her classmates. We would let God worry about what she did or didn't understand. Liz dutifully received Communion that day and every Sunday since. It doesn't really matter to her if you know why you do some things. You just do them because you're supposed to. If you're Catholic, you go to Communion. End of story.

Because she performed so well in some areas, I thought that maybe, with a little time, Lizzie really might catch up to her peers. In light of the fact that she already had excellent reading and math skills, I thought that possibly, if she repeated first grade, her language would continue to develop and she could spend her time catching up with the other kids in the subjects that were so hard for her, like social studies and science. I convinced the teachers and principal that it might help Lizzie to repeat first grade, and the request was submitted and granted. Of course now I realize that her language processing problem wasn't one that would go away with time, but then I didn't know what would help and no one in the education system had any better advice. Twenty-seven years later Liz still rakes me over the coals for making her "flunk" first grade. I'm absolutely sure she will never forgive me.

I watched closely during Lizzie's grade school years, hoping to see signs that she was closing the gap between herself and her peers, but in fact it was widening. It wasn't that she didn't make progress, she always did and still does, but progress was slow and never got her anywhere near other kids her age. There is an image that sticks in my mind of the neighborhood kids riding their two-wheelers up to the convenience store, while Lizzie trailed behind, pedaling for all she was worth to keep up on a bike with the training wheels still attached.

Liz was perfectly behaved at school. She never caused a problem. I don't think she ever spoke up. One of the few times teachers heard her voice was in reading group where she read circles around her classmates. Consequently the teachers thought she was capable of solving the thought problems and writing the book reports that were assigned. Bless her obsessive little heart, when Lizzie had a homework assignment, there was no way she was going to return to school the next day with it unfinished. Bob and I did our best to help her rather than doing the work for her, but she just didn't get it; and as the hour grew late and everyone's nerves frayed, we gave her the answers and tried to make her understand how we had arrived at them.

I've copied below part of a third grade reading comprehension worksheet, which was the kind of assignment Bob and I would help Lizzie with almost every night during her grade school career. I've highlighted the words whose meanings we would have to explain to Liz, even today, before she could begin to answer comprehension questions

The Butterfly

> Over grassy meadows
> Beneath the clear blue sky
> Through golden rays of sunlight
> Drifts the lovely butterfly
> She sways her slender body
> As gentle as a breeze
> Cheerful in her freedom flight

With pure and simple ease
Her beauty shimmers brightly
With colors all aglow
Feelings of peacefulness
Are only hers to know
Once a fuzzy creature
Without beauty and grace
She now flies so elegant
In all of time and space

http://www.ncsu.edu/project/lancet/third.htm

By the time we had gone over the meaning of all of these words and then tried to make sense of the phrases for Lizzie, it was well past bedtime (ours). At that point trying to plow through the comprehension questions was an exercise in futility.

At the conference before the beginning of each school year, most teachers were convinced that Lizzie could do much more than I gave her credit for. I would try to convince them that she really didn't understand what they were talking about or what she was reading – that her language processing difficulties stood directly in the way of comprehension. They would tell me that they were sure she understood more than I realized. Left unspoken was the assumption that it was just when Lizzie was with me that she didn't get it. They essentially thought my low expectations were the only obstacle to her writing a dissertation on the Big Bang Theory. Typically, when we met again at fall conference time, the teachers allowed as how maybe Lizzie wasn't getting everything that was said to her and maybe, just maybe, I wasn't crazy.

Sixth grade was the last time Liz's primary assignment was the regular classroom. When we assembled for the IEP meeting to transition from middle school to junior high, I told the IEP team that Lizzie was drowning in the regular curriculum and that for junior high I wanted her in a self-contained special education classroom within the school with some inclusion in the regular classroom. They mumbled uncomfortably about not knowing what the Central Office would say about that.

The words "Central Office" replaced for me the dreaded words from my childhood, "Permanent Record." Every child educated in the 1950's listened while teachers spoke in hushed and threatening tones of our Permanent Records. Every tardy, absence, disrespectful comment, every illicit visit with a neighbor was recorded on the Permanent Record to be expunged only at the time of the final confession. Like a bad penny, it could turn up at any time. Apparently every employer, college admissions office, teacher, and maybe even the FBI has a copy of my Permanent Record, but I will never be allowed to see it.

As intimidating as those two words had been for me, "Central Office" carried much more weight in my life as Liz's mom. I began to suspect that it wasn't the IEP team but the Central Office that really made all the decisions about the special education experience for a student. If the IEP team decided the child needed two hours a week of speech therapy, the Central Office could whittle those hours down to a wave hello from the speech pathologist as she passed by the classroom. If a parent suggested that the placement determined by the staff didn't seem to be in the best interests of her child and proposed an alternative, it would have to be cleared with the Central Office.

I informed the team in my best 'You might want to re-think this' voice that the law required that Liz's placement be determined by her needs, not the needs of the Central Office. Liz's needs were to survive junior high and that could not happen with her changing teachers and classrooms eight times a day while studying a curriculum that might as well have been presented in Vulcan. They talked about inclusion and how important it was to all students. I agreed that, in theory, including all children in the regular classroom was the ideal way to educate. However, in Liz's case, inclusion had meant years of frustration at going to school every day not understanding the instruction or what was going on around her, not to mention having no friends. Despite best practices and political correctness, I would not sacrifice Liz on the altar of a theory that did not work for her. I stood firm, and Liz began junior high in a special education classroom.

I was optimistic that things would begin to go easier for Liz, but in no time we were right back to business as usual. She was still being assigned science and social studies reports on topics that related to her world in much the same way that quantum physics does mine. At the first junior high IEP meeting I suggested that I thought it was not the best use of anyone's time to have Liz study the Spanish Explorers for the third year in a row. I was told that the Central Office required all students to conform to the school district's Instructional Objectives, even those students who didn't know what "explore" meant, hadn't the foggiest notion of what or where Spain was, and probably needed to explore how to get from here to there on a bus rather than how Columbus got from Spain to the new world on a the Santa Freakin' Maria. I was hard-pressed to find the Individualized in that Education Plan. When I mentioned to one of Liz's teachers that her dad and I were the ones who got an 'A' in Social Studies because we did all her homework so she'd have something to turn in, the teacher didn't bat an eye. It didn't seem to matter who got the grade as long as a grade was got.

In the meantime Liz and I both shed plenty of tears. I used to go to the library and get the easy reading level books for her research, like <u>My First Book About Pilgrims</u> or <u>My First Book About George Washington.</u> She would read from them (no problem) and then I would ask her what she had learned that she might put in the book report (big problem). Once, when she just couldn't understand the abstract ideas I was trying to help her write down, we both started to cry in frustration. I asked her if she could tell me what the problem was – did she not understand what I was saying or did she understand, but forget? For the first time, I got a glimpse into how Liz's brain functioned. She said that she thought she understood what was said to her for a second, but lost it before it got into her head. Remembering that night always brings on fresh tears when I think of Liz's frustration and my powerlessness to fix this misfire inside her brain. Liz tries so hard to understand things that come easily to the rest of us. She reads something almost every day from the newspaper because she wants to be informed like everyone else about what is going on in the world. Often she asks me about something in an article because, she can't, as she says, seem to "hold on to the idea" long enough to analyze it. I know it is enormously frustrating for her, but she never stops trying. And she never feels sorry for herself. She is my hero.

I have vivid memories of some of Liz's grade school teachers. Bob and I walked into Open House night when Liz was in second grade and introduced ourselves as Liz's parents. The teacher allowed as how Liz was one of her best students. I asked if she didn't think that might be because Liz had done first grade twice and consequently probably had the first few weeks of second grade locked. The teacher was not aware that Liz had repeated first grade because, as she proudly explained, she never read students' records. She was apparently concerned about the undue influence other professionals' observations would have on her opinion and she wanted to form her own. Call me crazy, but I think that knowing a child has repeated a grade could be kind of important when forming an opinion about how to approach teaching her, not to mention the fact that Liz had an IEP, which the teacher was legally obligated to follow. I suggested that this one time she might want to crack open the permanent record so we could all be on the same page about what we wanted Liz to accomplish in the coming year.

There was a particularly ugly incident when Liz was in second grade that did not involve her teacher. She had to take the bus to school that year because of court ordered integration. Every morning she went outside and stood on the corner to wait for the bus. At the same time her dad, clad in a black trench coat, drove out of the garage and pulled up to the corner in his rusted out, 10-year old car. He waited with Lizzie until the bus appeared in his rearview mirror, whereupon he pulled a little way up the street, waited until he was sure she was safely aboard, and drove on to work. On some mornings, he headed straight for the police department to review the cases of people who had been arrested overnight (like possibly, his wife), to determine what charges to file. On this morning, when he walked up to the counter to ask for the overnight sheets, he was met with gales of laughter from the police officer on duty. "What are you doing hanging around on street corners stalking little girls, you perv?" Bob had no idea what he was talking about. Eventually, the officer explained that they had received a call about a suspicious looking man, wearing a black trench coat, driving a beat up car, parked beside a little girl waiting on the corner across from our house. The caller, a woman from up the street who didn't know us, said that as soon as the bus appeared, the guy took off. Luckily she got his license number and turned him in. I will always be grateful to that caller for caring enough to watch out for a little girl she didn't even know and also for giving me the leverage I needed to talk Bob into finally junking that horrible car.

I was beginning to wonder if other families whose kids had disabilities ran afoul of the law as often as we did.

Liz had a bit of a crush on her fourth grade teacher and was quite interested in how she wore her hair. Once when I was cleaning her bedroom, I came across a notebook. I looked inside and saw that it was a diary of sorts. Each page had a date at the top. I was excited. Even though I probably shouldn't have been snooping, I thought the journal might provide some insight into how Liz felt about things in her life. Eagerly I turned the pages and on each one was written some variation of, "She wore her hair up today." Or "She wore it down long today." The coif report went on like that for about a month and then deteriorated into, "Up." "Down." "Down." "Up." "Up." "Up." I felt like I had stepped into the scene from "The Shining" where we get to see the book Jack Nicholson has been working on. It is filled with hundreds of pages of "All work and no play makes Jack a dull boy." I was worried that I might have the beginnings of a homicidal maniac on my hands. As it turned out, descriptions ended around the middle of October. I think Liz was getting bored with them. I was quite relieved.

Liz's fifth grade teacher was one of the most gifted educators I have ever observed. While Liz was in Mrs. S.'s class, she was to spend some of her time in the regular classroom and be pulled out for extra help in the special education resource room. The special education resource teacher at that school that year wasn't very effective. God bless Mrs. S., the regular classroom teacher, who saw this right off. She said at the IEP meeting that Liz wouldn't be going to the resource room too often. "I'm protective of my students' time in the classroom and I wouldn't want Liz to miss too much." I could have hugged her on the spot. Fifth grade was one of the best experiences of Liz's school life.

There was just one small hiccup. One night I was out for the evening and Bob was helping Liz with a social studies assignment. After a completely frustrating few minutes, he dialed up Mrs. S., who happened to be a personal friend of ours, and said, "You have to help me out. Jean's gone tonight and I'm helping Liz with her homework about Christopher Columbus. She says she's supposed to make a list of everything she doesn't know about him. Are you serious?" When her laughter subsided enough that she could speak, Mrs. S. said the assignment was to write down three things Liz would *like* to know about Chris. Bob said that after she explained the assignment, she started laughing wildly again and just hung up the phone. This teacher became a faithful, lifelong friend to Liz. She has remembered Liz's birthday ever since she was 10 years old.

In Liz's words . . .

"I can remember learning long division, fractions, measurements, which was hard, addition, subtraction, multiplication, and division facts in math, and long division had gotten easier as time went on, fractions I was somewhat great at, though it was difficult, and measurements was always hard, and all math facts of addition, subtraction, multiplication, and division, I learned pretty fast, and know it pretty well even today, except borrowing in subtraction, with zeros and nines, of when you change or don't change a zero that changed to a ten, again to a nine, and usually with this difficult piece of math, I either try subtracting and borrowing right, and see if it comes out right, or have the calculator figure it out for me.

In social studies, the 50 state capitals were taught, and a test was taken on the 50 state capitals, but it was multiple choice, to match the state with which state capital you think or know the capital of that state is. Some capitals were easy to know what the capital to that state is. For example, Honolulu is the capital of Hawaii, and the easiest way to remember the capital of Hawaii was to remember its capital starts with the same letter as that state, and the other 49 states, of some way to remember what its capital is, as capitals are pretty tricky and challenging to not get tricked what the capital of that state was after the test was taken.

I and the other kids in my class, also was able to write a report on any state of the other 49 states, excluding Nebraska. Mrs. S. knew that I had been to Colorado the most times out of any other state, and that I knew the most history on Colorado to write my report on that state, and she came to me first in class to let me write mine on Colorado, before someone else in class had taken Colorado to write theirs on.

Mrs. S. was the best teacher I ever had because she made the teaching and learning easy for me, she split my homework to sometimes do even numbers only, odd numbers only, or 1-15, or some type of splitting homework for me in English, and Math, and if I still had trouble with homework to come back the next day and say why what was incomplete was incomplete, and she would understand and go through with me what I had trouble with.

Since my 5th grade year, I've stayed in contact with Mrs. S., and had written letters telling how school was after I left her class. She has always sent my birthday card and still sends my birthday card every birthday I had since I left 5th grade, and she always sends and has sent my holiday card every holiday season, and she's been and still is my special friend

The other kids in my class, almost all were nice, and one of my best classmates was K. A. I can remember she was in my 3th through 6th grade class, and she would call me before school started in all four grades asking me what teacher I had gotten. I could remember what a nice, and kind friend she was in class and all the years I've known her.

K. L. was another classmate in my class, and she was always kind and nice, and we both went to resource class. K. remembers me being so nice and handling other kids with strength beyond my years, and I remember this about me when she told me this fact about me on Facebook that I wouldn't have thought of otherwise myself.

Another classmate I can remember is E. B., and E. was always a nice and kind boy; he always makes conversation, he's outgoing, he likes being around other people, I still see him time to time today because he is also a friend of Jackie's., a friend of my mom's from high school, and even when I still see him time to time, he's always fun to be around, to tell how things have been in his and my lifetime, and he's just a good kid."

Worth Keeping

The sixth grade teacher was renowned for her strictness. She felt duty bound to prepare her students for what was then called junior high – no exceptions. I knew Liz was struggling from the beginning, but Mrs. B. kind of scared me, so Bob and I dug in and helped her get the homework done every night and more or less waited for spring. When it came time for conferences, I approached the classroom with trepidation. Mrs. B was a very tall, stern looking woman. We made our introductions and she began to tell me what Liz couldn't do. I already knew what she couldn't do, and was waiting for the part about how it was probably my fault. I was taken aback when Mrs. B. said in her tall, stern voice, "So, I don't know what to do about Liz." I felt like she was going to hold me personally responsible for ruining her record of perfectly prepared sixth graders. I could feel my Irish getting up and was trying to figure out how I was going to respond without questioning the woman's ability, training, intent, religious beliefs and cooking skills. Before I could speak she added, "When I go home at night, I feel like I have failed Liz. I don't know how to help her." The air went out of my balloon just a moment before it exploded. We were immediately on the same page. I told Mrs. B. that if she or I could figure out the answer to Liz's problems, we would be rich women. The ice broken, we set a few simple goals that we could all work on for the remainder of sixth grade.

One thing Liz did right on schedule, at least for kids in our family, was to get a paper route in the sixth grade. Bob had been a paper boy and regaled us ad nauseum with the direct relationship between strength of character, honesty, industriousness and ultimate success in life, and being a paper carrier. Liz approached this job with the same precision she did every task. She performed it in the exact same way and to perfection every time. When the weather was bad, I would drive her to the start of the block where she would get out and deliver the papers to each house. I met her at the end of the block and drove her to the next stop. The first time I did this I was surprised to see that she walked right up to the door of each house and set the paper down. None of the happy-go-lucky flinging I had seen on TV shows. Sometimes, if she hadn't laid the paper down exactly right, she went back and adjusted the placement until it was completely squared up with the door jamb.

Apparently the paper carrier's handbook (according to Bob Sigler) explains that one should write a nice note to the customers at Christmas time, thus encouraging generous tipping during this season of good will. Over the years of her route, Liz's Christmas notes ran the gamut from veiled threats:

Dear Customer,
Happy Thanksgiving & Merry Christmas! Every year I always write a nice holiday letter telling you to have a fun holiday with your family and friends. This may be my last year delivering

your paper, it might not. At Thanksgiving I hope you know and remember what you are thankful for. (one thing you are thankful for is that I deliver your paper everyday and keep it dry in bad weather) At Christmas I hope you receive nice gifts, some that you want and some that you need. Again have a great Thanksgiving, a Merry Christmas, and a Happy 1999 New Year!
    Sincerely, Lizzie

to blame shifting:

Dear Customer,
Merry Christmas & a Happy New Year. I hope you'll like all the presents you receive from your family I've enjoyed delivering your paper for the last 2 ½ years even though I may have accidentally skipped you because either I thouht I gave you a paper, I put the paper in the mailbox, you just didn't look etc. I've also appreciated you giving me a call that I didn't give you a paper because I've gotten complaints where people complain that they didn't get a paper because they think it's not there when it is somewhere on their porch. Another reason why they complain is because they are used to where the paper lands when I deliver and then when I deliver with my dad on the weekends, he throws the paper from the bottom of the steps and it lands either on the porch where they can't find it or it lands in the bush, and then he has to get it out of there and keep throwing it until it lands on the porch. Again have a Merry Christmas & a Happy New Year.
Sincerely,
Lizzie Sigler

to the poor little match girl:

"Thank you for the tip. I wouldn't be able to buy my family Christmas gifts if I didn't get tips from my customers."

to the guilt trip:

"Thank you for your Christmas tip. Some gave $5, others, $20."

This last one inspired a couple of re-dos as people who were afraid to be outed as the neighborhood Grinch snuck onto our porch and slipped envelopes into our mailbox with an extra $5 or $10 in them.

Another of Liz's pastimes during her years of middle school was Girl Scouts. She had a fabulous leader who was willing to work with me on adapting the requirements for badges. Liz and I worked on each one and with some changes and a lot of help, she earned each badge right up to and including the Gold Award. It didn't hurt that she had won the prize for the most cookies sold, four years in a row. When selling season began, Liz would go door to door in our neighborhood and, of course, she sold to her family. The real blitz, though, came on the day I would drop her at the courthouse where Bob worked. She spent the day visiting lawyers, judges, secretaries and bailiffs. By the time she had filled all of their orders, she had sold upwards of 500 boxes. One year, a would-be competitor's father put a cookie order form on an office bulletin board. Bob immediately covered it with a note saying, "I will be here on Thursday to discuss your cookie needs." signed Lizzie Sigler

Is This Your Final Answer?

Toward the end of Liz's eighth grade year, a school psychologist called me at work. She said she had started to conduct the three-year reevaluation for Liz, but was unable to finish. She apologized and said she thought that both of them were having bad days and the testing hadn't gone well. She wanted to schedule another test date. I didn't ask what had happened, but I did ask her if she thought that her training as a school psychologist prepared her to evaluate and diagnose someone like Liz. Her response was, "No." I asked her, off the record of course, if she thought I should have Liz evaluated by an outside agency. She said, "Yes." She said that Liz didn't quite fit any of the conventional disability categories. We talked some more and, instead of rescheduling Liz for further testing by the public schools, I decided to have her tested by an outside agency.

It was about this time that people had started to become very interested in autism. A lot of research had been done and many folks who had been thought to have moderate to severe mental retardation or behavior problems were re-diagnosed as autistic. I had always been interested in autism and had done a lot of reading about it when I was a teacher. Some of the things Liz did from the time she was a baby made me think she might have autism, but she was so much higher functioning than any kids I had ever run into that I didn't think that could be the right diagnosis. At one point, I asked a colleague if she thought there might be such a thing as 'a little bit autistic.' We both thought there must be. Now we call it Asperger's Syndrome or Autism Spectrum Disorder.

I spoke to a woman I worked with on many committees. She had a son with autism, and said I should take Liz to the University of Iowa to be tested. They were doing a lot of work with kids who had autism and she thought they would be able to give us some answers. I scheduled an appointment and Bob and I drove Liz to Iowa City early one morning. We had been told to be prepared for about four hours of testing.

Eight hours and five batteries of tests later we gathered for the "staffing" with the team of eight professionals who had evaluated Liz. Each one summarized his or her findings, answered our questions, and made suggestions for teaching strategies. We asked what the consensus diagnosis was and were told that the team thought Liz had Pervasive Developmental Disorder Not Otherwise Specified (PDD\NOS). So this was our answer – a completely ambiguous phrase that doesn't explain anything? My response to this news was, "Huh?" One of the professionals answered my astute question by saying that in 10 years or so there would probably be a more descriptive and definitive term for what Liz has. He said that if we had brought her in when she was two or three, she probably would have been labeled autistic, but at 14, she didn't exhibit enough of the markers for that diagnosis. I was a little embarrassed when Bob asked this team of highly educated specialists who do nothing but evaluate children all day every day if they had ever seen anyone like Liz. When they answered, "No," the condescending smile disappeared from my face in a flash. One thing you do not want to hear from your daughter's medical\psychiatric\psychological/speech\educational professionals is that you have a one-of-a-kind kid.

By this time, Bob and I were on total overload and Liz was about to fold her tent, so we gathered all the reports and set sail for home. Bob admitted to feeling completely overwhelmed. I had a different reaction. This whole idea of Liz having some kind of autistic-like condition made more sense than any of the previous diagnoses. For me there was some comfort in having a label that carried with it descriptions, predictions and recommendations.

Even though it sounded like a catch-all, most of what I have read about PDD-NOS fits Liz. When I do a checklist comparing her behavior to the list of PDD-NOS characteristics, she matches up to most of them.

- *They may appear unemotional or unable to speak*

  Liz often has a flat affect. Her responses are frequently given in a monotone.

- *They could have trouble holding eye contact*

  This has always been hard for Liz

- *They may have trouble transitioning quickly from one activity to the next*

This was a big problem for Liz when she was a young child. I didn't tell her about tentative plans until we were almost ready to leave the house, just in case they changed, because change always sent her into a tizzy. She blamed me for spoiling her plans, as if I controlled the weather or other people's schedule adjustments. She still has difficulty with spontaneous changes of plans. When I suggested recently that we detour to the mall and do some shopping, she said she didn't have her money with her. I told her she could borrow from me and pay me back later. Her answer was that she really wasn't planning on that. This response has always meant, "I can't switch gears this quickly." She added that she had money, but it was at home. Since we were close, I drove her by the house and let her run in and get her own money. It is times like these when I realize how much she is at the mercy of what other people think she should do rather than what is logical to her, so I try to do what I can to give her some control over her life whenever possible.

- *They may have difficulty socializing with others*

  This is probably the most noticeable of Liz's autistic characteristics.

- *They may have heightened sensitivities to certain stimuli*

Once, when her brothers and dad and I were all laughing uproariously at something, I looked over at Liz and saw that she had tears in her eyes. I asked her if our laughing upset her and she said yes. I asked her why, but she wasn't able to tell me.

- *Some children get a seizure disorder such as epilepsy by their teen years*

Liz has partial complex seizures although she hasn't had one for over five years now. Her doctor is slowly withdrawing her from Phenobarbytol and so far, so good.

- *Teenagers often become depressed and have a lot of anxiety, especially if they have average or above-average intelligence*

66

Liz struggled with depression off and on from her teens to her late twenties. She would sit for hours staring at nothing and didn't seem to get much joy from anything. She took an anti-depressant for a few months, but it didn't seem to make much of a difference, so she stopped. Then, about three years ago, the depression disappeared suddenly.

Sometimes Liz gets overly anxious over small things. Frequently, when she is anxious or excited, she laughs to herself for long periods of time. I thought that maybe I should look into medication to help Liz control the laughing spells. I called five psychiatrists and all of their gatekeepers said that the doctors wouldn't be able to see her either because their practices were full or because of the PDD-NOS diagnosis. Liz said she didn't want to take another pill anyway. She says she knows she laughs too much sometimes and she thinks of things "like 9/11 or Hurricane Katrina" to make herself stop. She felt that was a better solution than taking another medication. She is her own medical guardian, so I respected her wishes and stopped my pursuit of a psychiatrist. Still it makes me feel sad to think of her having to keep a collection of tragic thoughts at the ready so she can stop inappropriate laughing

- *Ritualistic behavior involves an unvarying pattern of daily activities, such as an unchanging menu or a dressing ritual*

Liz used to limit her food preference to one kind at a time. She ate tuna salad almost exclusively for a couple of years and then didn't touch it for many more years. She has done that with many foods. She eats a greater variety of foods now, but once a food is off her list it generally stays off.

- *Relating to others*

She primarily relates to others in terms of her life and talking about herself, often in long monologues. That isn't to say she isn't interested in other people. She spends hours on Facebook finding out about friends and family and loves to report about them. Sometimes she just forgets to ask others about themselves. She's working on it.

- *Difficulty playing with others*

When she was six or seven and playing hide and seek with her brothers and some other kids, she didn't want to be "it." The rules of the game eluded her, and the other kids cried foul when Liz wouldn't take her turn. In their minds she was old enough to understand the rules, and they were giving no quarter. Lizzie refused to retreat to the counting tree and chaos ensued. I took her inside and tried to explain to her that she had to take her turn being "it" if she wanted to play. She bellowed and howled for half an hour, but I wouldn't let her outside until she agreed. By the time she gave in, the game was over.

Now here is where Annie Sullivan would be able to report that Helen learned a valuable lesson and ever after played with other children in perfect harmony. I don't know what Liz learned for sure. I'm never quite sure. She probably would have remembered that you have to be "it" if you want to play hide and seek with the other kids, but the lesson would not have carried over to other games. Learning is a step at a time experience for Liz and she doesn't transfer the rules of one game over to another and certainly not to the game of life. As I said, Annie I'm not.

- *Problems with two-way conversations*

She often rambles without pause for many minutes at a time. The listener has little opportunity to respond.

- *Rigid range of interests for social interaction*

She engages in a narrow range of activities and usually talks about the same subjects over and over. Add poor language processing to this list and you have a pretty accurate description of Liz's challenges

In Liz's words . . .

What it is like to have PDD, which stands for Pervasive Developmental Disorder, is really pretty simple. All it is is a language disorder, of trouble understanding language what is being said in conversation, or how things are worded in the

paper, books, or paperwork of applications for employment, doctors and dentists offices, or anything that contains words. I usually understand things when I've reread it a few times, and anything said or worded, if it's reworded in a way I understand, it becomes more easier to understand what was worded in a different way, It is also a slight disability, as I'm also a fast learner in counting money and change in several different combinations it's still the same amount of money, writing checks, balancing bank statements, I know roman numbers, I know how to read non digital time where hands point to the numbers what time it is, and all the things I know because I'm so bright and intelligent, and how fast I learn things. I don't find it has made my life much more difficult. It would have been harder if I would have had Down Syndrome or Cerebral Palsy. I don't find mine made it a complicated life. I see many kids with disabilities who can't learn as fast as me.

The End of Inclusion

While I was researching PDD and autism, unbeknownst to me two of my friends, Jackie and Linda, who by that time had nurtured Liz and me for 14 years, were doing some research of their own. A few weeks before we went to the University of Iowa, I had been telling them about my worries about Liz and they were trying to be positive and good friends and were saying sweet, encouraging things about her, like: nobody but me noticed there was anything wrong; she was just fine; the out of control rages that were becoming more and more frequent (but only at home) were just an aspect of her personality; I expected too much from her because her brothers were so smart; and so on. I knew how much they cared about Liz and me, but all of a sudden something snapped and I said (maybe yelled just a little), "You know, I appreciate that you are trying to make me feel better, but Liz isn't fine. There is something wrong and I can't go on like this trying to make the two of you feel better by pretending. Every time I have to rehash her problems with you to try to convince you that I'm not crazy, it hurts! I need your support, not pie in the sky!" I think I finally made my point.

The next time we went out to dinner, the girls made it clear that they had indeed heard me. They announced that they had gone to visit the Madonna School for Exceptional Children and thought it would be the perfect place for Liz. I was slack-jawed! I looked at them like they were crazy and nuts not to mention clueless. "Madonna is for kids with Down Syndrome and mental retardation! Lizzie wouldn't fit in there. That's a terrible idea!"

The Madonna School had been founded by a dynamic ball of fire in a nun's habit. Sister Evangeline was something of a legend in Omaha. In disability circles you only had to say "Sister" and people knew who you were talking about.

My friends were prepared for my argument. They told me that Sister had quite a few students enrolled who had nothing more serious than Learning Disabilities. There was a student council, a prom, a sweetheart dance, and Special Olympics sports teams. All of this sounded wonderful. Liz hadn't been involved in any school activities for several years. She didn't have friends except in the neighborhood, and they had begun to pull away as they got into their pre-teen years. The idea that she could have some semblance of a normal high school experience was so tempting that I almost forgot that we were talking about The Madonna School for "Exceptional" Children, the 1970s euphemism for kids with intellectual disabilities.

"You don't understand. This would be taking a giant step backward for Liz. These separate schools are about as politically incorrect as you can get these days. It's all about all kids blending in together in regular schools and regular classrooms. For God's sake, I give workshops on Inclusion and how it should work for every child!" Linda looked into my eyes and said in her most supportive, loving way, "And how's that been working for Lizzie so far?"

When I looked back over Liz's school career, I knew Jackie and Linda were right. Most of the classwork was over her head. She had never fit in or been accepted by her peers, but now she was beginning to notice. She was floundering in junior high. Despite our best efforts, she was not getting the support she needed scholastically or socially. She would come home in tears and tell me some of the things the other kids said. A memory that is even more gut wrenching for me than seeing Liz go to kindergarten on a special education van is seeing her standing in front of me sobbing and asking me, "Why do they want to be cruel to someone?" I couldn't think of an answer to her question. I still can't.

Reluctantly I agreed to give the Madonna School some thought. I did a lot of soul searching. I visited and spoke with Sister and she convinced me that it would be a great place for my daughter and that Liz would by no means be the highest functioning student there. I took Liz for a visit and thought she would comment on the kids with Down Syndrome (because that is such a visible thing), but she didn't. In fact, in all the years she attended Madonna, she never mentioned the fact that most of the kids had mental retardation. We enrolled Liz for the following school year. She thrived in that environment for the next seven years. She had friends, was elected to student council, and was crowned queen of some dance or other. She talked on the phone for hours every day night. It was so exciting to get Liz her own phone line just like any other teen-aged girl. She and three or four other girls from school held conference calls where they discussed events of the day, other kids, and appropriate behavior. From my end of the conversation, it seemed like the appropriate behavior discussions were usually led by Liz and were more of a tyrannical lecture (she being the tyrant) than a dialogue about society's rules, but the group never seemed to tire of the lectures and debates.

As a reward for some accomplishment, Sister had a friend of hers teach Liz how to latch hook rugs. That took care of the bulk of her down time for all of the Clinton years. She must have hooked about 275 rugs. Once Liz started a rug, she stopped only for brief naps and the occasional meal. As soon as she finished a rug, she started a new one. If you are a friend of Liz's and live in the greater metropolitan Omaha area, you have a latch hook rug. If she ever gets married, I'm going to ask for all of the rugs back so I can line them up in the center aisle of the church instead of the white satin runner. I have no doubt the rugs would go out the front door and around the block.

During her years at Madonna, Liz was introduced to another pastime that fills many of her leisure hours today -- Special Olympic sports. Sister mandated participation by all students in all sports. That meant basketball, track, bowling and swimming. It looked great on the brochures and Sister was nothing if not an accomplished fundraiser. I will always be grateful to Sister Evangeline for providing Liz with some ways to fill her off-work hours. She continues to play on a Special Olympics basketball team and goes to every Creighton basketball game. Above all else, she has bowling.

In Liz's words...

My activity of bowling is and has been one of my favorite things to do since I was 22. I started at that age going to bowling weekly for competing with Special Olympics, and summer league in the summer. I also go and have gone bowling with my dad since I was 22 also after church at 10:00-11:00 at a bowling alley which has *an hourly special to go bowling on Sunday mornings for an hour for $9.50, which is pretty cheap.*

My dad taught me bowling also, and I was taught how to release my throw, to bend over and release, and to throw straight, and most of the time I'll get strikes on most of my throws, otherwise I usually get my spares if I don't get a strike on the first throw. My consistency has improved as I learned bowling, and I break great high 100 games about every week, usually from anywhere in the 140's or better. I've also broken 200 a number of times over the years, and I usually break 200 a few times throughout the whole year. Some of my scores over 200 I've broken are 200 even, 203, 217, 225, and other great over 200 scores. I've broken games in the 170's to the 190's, and I've broken a 171, 175, 179, 183, 187, 189, 191, 193, 197, 198, and 199, and other scores I've broken close to 200.

I've gone bowling with my Uncle Denny and Aunt Denise in Denver on some of their trips here in town, I've gone bowling with my mom's cousin Kathy, I've gone bowling with my brother David in Providence, and my niece, Isabel, and my nephew Jake, I've gone bowling with my godmother Martha in Denver, I've gone bowling with my godmother's son Tim. Omaha, I've gone bowling with my friend Suzy and her husband Joey, in Denver, I've gone bowling with my Aunt Mary and my cousin Trish in Iowa, I've gone bowling with Best Buddies with Creighton kids as a group

event one month of the academic year, and I've gone bowling with
my college buddy as a one on one plan, and has always been fun.

Last year, Liz's email was hacked into and someone sent a nasty, dirty message to all of her contacts. Horrified, I immediately sent a follow-up message explaining that it wasn't actually Liz who had expressed the passion for sex. My niece wrote back saying, "Don't worry Aunt Jean, nobody would believe that was an email from Liz. There wasn't one mention of bowling or a 200 score."

As good as the Madonna experience was, it didn't bring about a cure. Liz's academic progress was about the same at Madonna, minus the frustration of trying – unsuccessfully - to learn a lot of useless (to her) information. She continued to struggle with reading comprehension and language processing. I continued having to convince teachers that she wouldn't be able to do things like get a GED. And although she had friends at school, she often remained aloof from them at social and sports gatherings. She preferred the company of her friends' parents and my friends to people her own age. Maybe it is because adults were more polite than her peers and didn't cut her off when she began a 10-minute monologue that probably had nothing to do with what had previously been said.

Still, taken as a whole our lives were a hundred times easier and happier during those years at a special school.

In Liz's words . . .

After 8th grade, which was way too hard in English, Social Studies, and about every class I went to, I went to Madonna School, where kids with learning problems\learning disabilities are sent there, and have gone there to get the learning I needed, and school there became much easier, better, and less frustrating than junior high and at the public schools, as the teachers I had knew what teaching and learning to give me. All the kids that went to school there were kind, nice, friendly, and they get along in class, at lunch, and at recess, and before and after school to socialize, and some kids that went to school in my class had Down Syndrome, or some type of problems in learning like mine was in, with the language disorder and autism.

There were student council events usually once a month at school or a few times a year during the academic year, all classes went swimming once a week on the day of the week their class swam in the afternoon, the oldest classes went to work a couple days a week half days usually mornings for ones working in the community, and school would transport the ones that had to work to their employer on the days they had to work, and they would come back to school by lunch.

Many kids were involved in Special Olympics, and they swam on swim team, played basketball, and ran track for school, and it was always fun, and getting involved in something new that you have never done or had been involved in before, and might not have gotten or wouldn't have gotten involved in otherwise. My class and the other class of the kids in the other class my age, went to Adventureland the end of school in May after Memorial Day or a day in June for a senior skip day event, and going to Adventureland for a day was so much fun and we came back the end of the evening to school to go home.

The teacher I graduated with, Mrs. L., was another of my best teachers I had, and she knew when I was having a hard week or some hard days at school to get me through it, she gave me the learning and teaching I needed, and it was hard leaving her teaching me coming to graduation, though I always have remembered and still remember the things about her when she taught me for two years. I'll never forget and always keep in mind what she told me how to deal with and handle things in life, and one of the things she always told me was to take it one step at a time when getting stressed, having a hard time or hard day at work, or anything I'm having to deal with to keep that tip in mind, and it has helped, and helps me a lot in times when I've been stressed.

The World of Work

As soon as Liz finished school, she and I went to the government office charged with helping people with disabilities find a job. Because of her disability, Liz was entitled to get help finding a job and to spend a certain number of months with a job coach who would help her learn the job. We sat in a tiny cramped office explaining to a nice gentleman what Liz's skills and abilities were and what kind of job might be suitable. He listened carefully, took notes, typed something into his computer, turned back to us and told us how much Liz would have to pay each month for services. I was confused. I had always thought these services were free and told the gentleman as much. I asked him how Liz was supposed to pay for help finding a job when she didn't have a job and therefore had no money to pay with. He told me that since she lived at home with us, our income had to be figured into the mix and the charges were based on that amount. I was flabbergasted and felt an obligation to let this representative of the bureaucracy know it. I told him that our family had never asked the government for anything beyond a free, appropriate public school for Liz. We had paid for private testing when we thought it was necessary. We had paid tuition for private education when the public schools couldn't meet Liz's needs. We had provided for all her needs because she was our child and that's what you do for your child. Now, however, Liz was an adult citizen of the state of Nebraska. It was time for Nebraska to kick in and do its part to help get her a job and become a tax-paying citizen. The nice gentleman said that wasn't how it worked any more. I told him that I understood and that he should be sure to watch the news that night where he would see me taking his boss, the head of Health and Human Services, to task on the air. I would then contact my senators and congressmen and tell them that in Nebraska, adult people with disabilities were being charged for services based on income that wasn't theirs. The nice man re-checked his computer, swung back around to us and said, "I think we'll be able to help Liz without charge."

A few days later, Liz got a call telling her that the agency had found her a job. She would be working at a Kinko's downtown making copies and such. I had reservations about Liz taking orders, remembering, and then carrying out those orders, as well as learning how to operate a variety of machines, but I was tired of telling people she couldn't do what they thought she could do and besides, I thought she deserved the chance to try. I should have listened to my instincts and stepped in. I should have told the case worker that the job was unsuitable for Liz and that he should keep looking, but I didn't. The experience was a disaster. People were placing orders at the furious pace of a downtown copy shop. Liz couldn't process what they were saying fast enough to get the orders down. She wasn't able to remember how to work the machines. People got impatient and yelled at her. The job lasted two weeks. It took Liz's ego a year to recover from the beating.

I learned something from this experience. I knew this job would be too difficult for her, but I didn't say anything. That was a mistake. I vowed that from that time on I would step in when I knew that Liz was about to get involved in a situation that she couldn't handle no matter how my interfering looked to other people. Her learning differences are subtle and sometimes, because of my 24\7 exposure to these differences, I am the only one who can see when something is going to be too hard for her. I am over worrying about people thinking she's fine and I'm crazy. Liz vowed she would never work with the public again.

A few weeks later a colleague of mine called and said, "You need to call this woman at Mutual of Omaha right away. I was just there with a client looking at a job. It wouldn't have worked for him, but I think it might be perfect for Liz and this woman is willing to meet with her." I called the number she gave me and set up a time for Liz to have an interview with the supervisor of the mailroom at Mutual's casualty insurance division. She said that she would be willing to try Liz out for the job. It involved sorting incoming mail, running address labels and preparing outgoing mail for the post office. Liz started the following week.

Much as I wanted to, I never called her supervisor to see how Liz was doing. I could hear her voice in my head asking, "Would you call David or Andy's boss? No, you wouldn't because they are adults. I'm an adult too and I'll handle my own business!" She must have done okay because she held that job for four years. Then suddenly she was notified that Mutual was no longer going to carry casualty insurance, and her job was eliminated.

Liz was out of work for a year. It was a very long year for her. When you have no job, can't drive, and don't read or watch TV, there are a lot of hours in the day. I looked online every week or so and I noticed an ad for a collating job. The job had to be accessed through an employment agency.

Now it must be said that Liz is hell on wheels at collating. When she was in school, she assembled pocket binders for workshops at a job training site. She did the same thing at the place where I worked. The repetition and structure of collating were perfect for her. Sometimes when I was behind on workshop folders, I would bring 50 of them home over the weekend along with sets of 30 or so handouts that had to be put in each of the folders. I would lay out the materials on the dining room table, and

Liz would gather them up and place them in the folders at lightning speed. She never stopped working until the last folder was complete. The only problem I had was that when she finished there were always a few handouts left over due to my careless counting practices, which she criticized with great regularity. No matter how I assured her that the fault was undoubtedly mine, Liz always thought that maybe she should go back and look through all 50 folders and each of the 30 handouts just to make sure she hadn't made a mistake. It took a lot of convincing, but I was able to talk her out of double checking with solemn promises that I would be a more careful counter next time.

In light of her collating record, I thought the job posted online might be perfect for Liz. I went with her to the employment agency. When her name was called, we both stood up. A woman introduced herself to Liz and asked her to step to the other end of the room. After a minute I walked over to the two of them and told the woman that Liz had a language problem, and sometimes had a little difficulty with job interviews and the exchange of facts. I told her that I would be happy to sit in on the interview to be sure that both of them got the information they needed. The woman took a step back and said, "If she can't understand then she can't do the job." I assured her that once the details were worked out and Liz had learned the job, there would be no further need for anyone to help her. Once she learns a job, that's it. Done deal. She will do that job correctly and until it is finished every time. I told the woman about Liz's four successful years at a more complicated clerical position, but she had made up her mind. "She can't do the job if she can't understand the directions." I told her that Liz would come complete with a job coach who would stay on with her until she and the employer were comfortable that Liz was ready to fly solo. The woman would not be moved. "Don't you have a policy for accommodations for people with disabilities?" I asked. She said they did not and that was the end of the discussion.

I was furious. We got in the car and I told Liz that what had just happened was wrong. She was a little confused, because things had moved pretty fast for her. I explained that the woman had assumed that she couldn't do a collating job because of her language processing problem. We both knew that wasn't true. The whole thing put me in mind of one of my favorite quotes. It came from Ollie Webb, a woman with mental retardation. She had been working for years at a country club in Omaha making sandwiches. When a new young manager came on board he decided that Ollie would have to be terminated because she didn't have a high school diploma. Ollie's comment on this judgment was, "You don't need a diploma to make no damn sandwiches!" She remained at the club long after the hot shot manager, a fact that she loved to share. In Liz's case, she didn't have to have great language skills to put together a damn sales folder. The woman at the employment agency had stepped all over the Americans with Disabilities Act in making that assumption. I asked Liz if she would be willing to file a complaint with the Equal Employment Opportunities Commission. She was very active in self advocacy at that time, and I told her I thought this was exactly what she had been practicing for. She agreed and with my help she filed a complaint.

The hearing was held and both sides told their story. The woman had lied to the representatives from her company and said that I had not told her that Liz had a disability. I knew enough about mediation to know that it wasn't a time for he said/she said, but it made me angry anyway. I kept my mouth shut though. After all the evidence had been presented, the mediator asked Liz and me what we were looking for in the way of recompense. Liz couldn't get any monetary compensation because there was no actual job loss involved at the point when the discrimination occurred. I said I would like to see the woman and the staff of the employment agency get training on the ADA and on the illegality of making unfounded assumptions about job performance based solely on the fact that an applicant has a disability. All parties agreed to this solution. Liz and I were satisfied that 20 or so people were going to have their collective consciousness raised at least a little bit. I was secretly chuckling at the thought of how those 20 people were going to feel about their co-worker's smug, unbending attitude causing them to give up a whole Saturday to attend a training session. Sounded like justice to me!

Lizzie at three months

Easter Sunday at Nana's house —
16 months old

Wearing the patch on her
lazy eye — four years old

A rare snuggle — Lizzie seven years old

In fifth grade classroom

Hands across America — Lizzie eight years old

Linda and I at the scene of the Old Mill crime

Liz with Linda (L) and Jackie (R)

Liz with her "Aunt" Martha

Liz's Friend Melanie

Liz with Robin and her son, Chad

Liz with Irene (L) and Rose (R)

Liz with her brothers, David (L) and Andy (R)

Liz with her aunt Barb and uncle Dufy

Liz with Nana

Challenger Little League

Special Olympics Track

Special Olympics Basketball

Bowling with Dad, Aunt Denise and Uncle Denny

2013

In Liz's words . . .

I had been discriminated against in September, 2004, for not being given the right to apply for employment. I went to apply for a job collating booklets, or collating that I have experience in when I have volunteered where my mom worked, and I volunteered to put mailings, and brochures of packets, and different things collated together, and I filled out the pre-application, turned it in, and had my name called to see me. The woman says I had misunderstood what was asked on the pre-application, because of how it was worded on the application I didn't understand because of the autism and the PDD I have. My mom and I asked her if the employer hires anyone with a disability, and the woman's response was if I can't fill out applications independently, then I can't do the job I'm applying for. My mom told the woman it was very discriminatory, and she and I walked out of the employer.

I then went to EEOC (Equal Employment Opportunities Commission) to file the complaint, and I told what I was discriminated against for. I signed papers, I had gotten all my documents copied when I was tested in Iowa, and everything I have on my file and records to file the complaint. When I filed the complaint, I was also given The Americans With Disabilities Act----Your Employment Rights As An Individual With a Disability book, that I still have and have saved, that if I would ever be discriminated against again and that also I can show other friends and family my discrimination rights book to tell and show how I was discriminated against for not being given the right to apply for employment.

At the mediation, my mom and I discussed that all employers should treat all applicants applying for employment fairly, whether they have or don't have a disability, all applicants have the right to apply for employment, and the woman found out a complaint was filed for discrimination that I filed myself, to teach her, everyone that works at that employer, and the employer itself, that I was discriminated against, and that I was given mistreatment. The discrimination complaint was resolved successfully, and the woman that discriminated against me learned a lesson from this. I learned to not go back to that employer again to try applying for employment a second time, after I had been discriminated against once, and I didn't want to be discriminated twice for the same reason.

During this time, I was in a Masters Swim Program at the local university. I was talking to my coach one day and the subject of Liz's job search came up. He said I should talk to the supervisor of the food service department at the university. He thought they hired people with disabilities to work in the student center. I made the call and set up an appointment for Liz to interview. She was hired and started a week later. She had some rough times at first. She started out on the buffet line dishing up food, but she kept putting the serving spoon back in the pan, in violation of a health code, instead of laying it alongside, so she was moved to stocking cupboards, refilling the cup holders and cleaning tables.

When she had been at the job for a couple of years, Liz came to me and told me with tears in her eyes that her supervisor wanted me to call. Liz wasn't sure what she had done, but I could tell that she was anxious and upset about it. She thought it might have something to do with the fact that when students asked her where something was she pointed out the sign that clearly told them where it was. She thought that might have made some of them mad. "Ya think?" ran through my head. I made the call and her supervisor told me that I had to explain to Liz that when a cup lid fell on the floor, she couldn't pick it up and put it back in the dispenser. I assured the woman that I would talk to Liz. I explained to Liz that there are millions of germs on the floor that get on the cup lid and can spread diseases to anyone who might put the lid on their cup. Her expression brought me back to the days of the social studies reports. I asked her if she knew what a germ was and she said no. I seem to remember that those Spanish explorers brought with them diseases that made the natives really sick. Seems like those social studies teachers could have snuck in the definition of a germ with that lesson. I guess it wasn't in the Instructional

Objectives. I gave her a brief lecture on contagion and sanitary food handling practices and told her I thought she would be fine, that if she were going to get the sack, they would have told one of us by now. Another year passed and I thought Liz was doing fine, but one day I got another call from her supervisor asking if I would come to the university and meet with her and Liz's boss. I said of course I would.

When I entered the Food Services office I was greeted by the head of the division, Liz's supervisor and, to my astonishment, the Vice Chancellor of the University. What could Liz possibly have done to upset the Chancellor? I was afraid maybe he had gotten sick from a dirty cup lid. Liz's boss said they all had concerns about Liz's attitude. Her behavior seemed rude and they had gotten complaints. The Vice Chancellor said that public perception of the university was at the top of the Chancellor's list of priorities. Apparently Liz had been rude to him and he was considering letting her go. I explained that a lot of what seemed rude behavior could be directly related to Liz's disability. Her supervisor said, "I'm not sure exactly what Liz's disability is." That opened the door for me to explain a lot about PDD and autism and that one of the main manifestations of it is poor social skills. I asked exactly what Liz was doing to offend people. They reported that she didn't smile and quickly walked away from people after brusquely answering their questions. She was lifting up students' belongings and wiping the table underneath. I was relieved in a way because these were things we could deal with. I explained to them that Liz didn't realize that walking so fast, not smiling and moving students' belongings were all considered inappropriate behavior, but that she could be taught. I assured them that she did not mean to be surly or impatient. I also explained that telling her the behavior was interpreted by others as rude was probably not enough. In Liz's mind, if she doesn't mean to be mean or rude or angry or bored, people should know that and not get mad at her. The best approach would be to point out the inappropriate behavior and describe to her exactly what she needed to do instead. I assured them that once she understood what she should do, she would do it. We talked for a long time, the three of them asking questions about PDD\autism and me answering them. By the end of the conversation they were all on Liz's team and promised to contact me if there were any further problems so I could explain things to Liz. Thank God Liz didn't get fired that day, but just as importantly, I was able to help three people and the Chancellor of an entire university understand some of the challenges Liz and people like her face each day. It felt good and I admire and am grateful to those people for making the effort to understand.

People have asked me if I think it would be easier if Liz's disability were something more obvious. Sometimes I think it would be. When I had finished explaining Liz's issues to the people at her job, her boss, with a little resentment in his tone, God bless him, said, "Some of the public school special ed kids who work here," (most with identifiable disabilities), "do a lot worse things than Liz and nobody says anything about them!" It was just another time that people's expectations were set unrealistically high because a lot of the time Liz looks and sounds like everybody else.

In Liz's words . . .

My employment at the copy shop didn't work out because I was put through a position of work I wasn't hired to do. I was supposed to make copies when needed, and instead I was put through cashiering and dealing with the public that I wasn't hired to do, and had to end my employment there because of it.

My employment at Mutual of Omaha when I worked there until I was laid off, was I worked in mail, and did clerical work of sorting the output out. Once a month, the agents would get their commission check, same thing as an employee getting their check every pay period. The commission checks had to be done on the 10th of every month, and if the 10th fell on Saturday or Sunday, the commission checks were done on the Friday before.

My employment with the university, I work in food services. I wipe counters, wipe down tables, switch out the trash, pick up trays all day on trash cans after they have been used, and brought into the dishroom to run through the dishwasher to bring the clean trays back out to the tray shelves, wipe down microwaves, refill drink cups, keep the cabinets full of the drink cups, refill the napkin dispensers so they don't run out, and when they have run out to refill it, refill the lid containers of the drink lids, refill the straw container of straws when running low, or there's room to fill some more. I keep the lids cabinet filled of lids, and the cabinet with the napkins and straws filled of napkins, and straws.

My employment at the courthouse, I work there in the summer, when school is out at the university until school starts in the middle of August to have some type of employment for summer. I help out with boxing terminated files, make copies of anything that needs copies made, pull files, shift files around on the file shelf that there's more room to get more files on there, and to loosen some of the tightness, I help make file folders of writing the attorney's name, the class number, what the count is, and all the information that has to be written on the file folders, help sort out files in numerical order for the law clerks to file the files on the shelf, shredding of any papers or documents or of anything to be put through the shredder, help collate packets, take rushes over to the juvenile court side, and any work to be done to help out for the summer. My employment I like better is the courthouse because I know everyone there, the employees are nice and get along with, I have the experience in filing, shredding, collating, making file folders, and all the work I help with. The pay is better, and it's a kind and pleasant environment to work in.

A New Career Path

My career took a couple of turns over time, but always stayed on the Special Education/Disability path. Right out of college I was a full time special education teacher for three years. Then when I got pregnant with my son David and had to take some time to deliver him, I was forced to resign my teaching job and was told I could reapply when I was ready to come back. It seems hard to believe now that I didn't immediately lawyer up, but the times were different. I made many frantic phone calls to the administration of the school system over that summer. I was informed that my job had been given to the substitute who had stepped in to fill my absence for the last three weeks of the school year when I had to leave suddenly to accommodate David's early arrival. They were looking for a suitable position for me and they would let me know as soon as they found something. About the middle of August I got a call asking if I would be interested in being a Special Education Resource teacher. The department was starting a new program and five of us would be the pioneers. It sounded like an interesting job and I accepted it. I was a Resource teacher for one year and then I quit working full time for a few years while my family increased and multiplied.

When Lizzie started all-day preschool, I did a lot of substitute teaching. I worked only in special education classrooms and the jobs were all challenging. In the best of circumstances a sub is smack dab in the middle of the crosshairs of even the most cooperative student. In a special education classroom many of the children have behavior issues. They don't accept change easily and some generally don't understand and\or care for rules. Some days, after a particularly difficult assignment, I wished I had chosen an easier career – maybe testing the ropes for that tribe in Africa I saw on PBS who bungee jump and land on their heads on purpose.

I spent seven years substitute teaching. The last job I ever had was a nightmare from hell. The kids cursed, slept, threw things, threatened me and each other, and made lewd suggestions involving most of my family members. When I got home that night, I told my husband that I would never teach again. I was never really suited to be a teacher; it is just that when I went to college, a girl became a nurse, teacher or social worker – whether or not she was cut out to be any of them.

The next day I looked in the want ads to see if I was equipped to do anything but teach. I saw an advertisement for The Nebraska Parent Training and Information Center (PTI). The ad said the agency served families of children with disabilities and that parents of children with disabilities would be given hiring preference. I called and scheduled an interview. The Director of this newly established agency began by saying, "As you know, there is a section in the IDEA that mandates a PTI in every state." I nodded knowingly, despite being completely ignorant about what the IDEA or a PTI was. She continued, "We are looking for someone to present trainings on the law and the state rule which, of course, won't come out until the regs come down. I allowed as how I thought that was a great plan - (What state rule? What regs? What *are* regs?). The job would involve traveling the length and breadth of the state of Nebraska presenting workshops. Well now, this job was almost irresistible. One can drive for 10 hours in Nebraska and still be in Nebraska. I have come close to scooping my eyeballs out from boredom when driving to Scottsbluff. As for public speaking – I had never done it. I said it sounded like a wonderful opportunity and I would bring all my years of experience to bear on this endeavor should she choose to hire me. She told me she would let applicants know her decision within a week.

I went home and found out that the IDEA is the Individuals with Disabilities Education Act. For the life of me, I don't know how I found that out without Google, but I did. I asked my lawyer husband what "state rule" meant and he told me the states establish their own rules for administering federal laws. That was all I learned. I didn't want to worry my pretty little head with excess information in case I didn't get the job. I had no reason to think I would get it, but a week or so later, the director called and asked me if I was still interested and offered me the job. I accepted.

For the first several months, all I did was study - federal law, state law, Health and Human Services policy, Medicaid rules, local special education policies. I read and read and read, preparing for the day when I would share my vast stores of knowledge with unsuspecting parents who thought I had some sort of clue. I was told that I and a couple of other trainers to be named later were going to begin presenting workshops in about five months' time. The only problem was the workshops hadn't been created yet. That would be the trainers' job. Luckily there were mature parent organizations from which the baby parent organizations could borrow workshops and revise them for their particular states. I began to write workshops. For me, writing a workshop consisted mainly of running a find-and-replace and changing the word Minnesota to Nebraska. Since the regs weren't down yet (I still wasn't quite sure what that meant), everything was pretty generic.

I was a trainer for about four years and then became the Director of the agency. I could spend a chapter or two talking about my work experiences, but I think there was something in a writing class I took about not boring the reader stupid. In a nutshell, I moved from being a trainer and then Director of the Nebraska Parent Center to becoming Executive Director of GOARC, the umbrella agency that held the Parent Center grant.

GOARC originally was an acronym for the Greater Omaha Association for Retarded Citizens. Sometime during the 1980s, people began to realize how offensive the word "retarded" was. Not only was it used as a pejorative in name calling and jokes, it was a meaningless blanket term used to describe millions of people who are as different from each other as the people in the general population are. So the ARCs (Associations for Retarded Citizens) across the country began describing themselves using "people-first" language. The philosophy behind people-first language is that people should be known by their names, not their disabilities, e.g., not the retarded guy, but Bill, a person with mental retardation; not "autistic" but a person with autism; not an agency who serves retarded people but people with mental retardation and other developmental disabilities.

The problem with using people-first language to describe GOARC was that whenever I went out to talk about the agency at a fundraising event, I spent the first five minutes explaining why the agency no longer used the name GOARC, that the acronym ARC had been replaced with the word Arc, which didn't stand for anything, and that the new name was the Greater Omaha Association for People with Mental Retardation and Other Developmental Disabilities. By that time, eyes began to glaze over and I was afraid I was going to lose them completely.

My development director and I came up with an idea. We got board approval to name the agency after Ollie Webb who had spent many years of her life in the state home in Beatrice, Nebraska. During the 1950s, there was a nationwide push to close state institutions like Beatrice and provide supports to people with mental retardation in their home communities. The days of warehousing people were over. With the help of many friends and organizations, Ollie was able to settle in Omaha where she lived out her life in a home that she owned and shared with other people who had developmental disabilities. Now I was able to explain that the Ollie Webb Center, which provides community-based supports, was named after a woman whose life moved from the hell of the state institution to being a landlady, world traveler, and advocate because of those supports. It seemed to make things a lot clearer. There is a video telling Ollie's remarkable story which can be seen on the Minnesota Governor's Council on Developmental Disabilities website: http://www.mnddc.org/

As with all the other labels and monikers in the disability field, terminology continues to change, but the word retarded will, thankfully, never be resurrected. I recently learned that Intellectual Disabilities is the newest preferred language replacing Developmental Disabilities. I am breathless trying to keep up. In her lifetime, Liz has been labeled Developmentally Delayed, Mentally Handicapped, Borderline, Language Disordered, Hyperlexic, a person with Pervasive Developmental Disorder Not Otherwise Specified, and, most recently, a person on the Autism Spectrum. I sometimes feel as if I should introduce her like Prince, "This is Liz, The Daughter formerly known as . . . ".

Thank you, dear readers, for your patience as you slogged your way through The Life and Times of Jean Sigler. I wanted to lay some groundwork before talking about the adult social programs which have become such a significant part of Liz's life. Liz has been involved in social and self-advocacy activities through the Ollie Webb Center since she was 16 years old. These programs have been a godsend for her. They keep her busy and active and involved with other people. Liz's life would be a solitary and lonely one if it weren't for these programs.

When Liz turned 15, Bob, a remarkably courageous man, made a valiant effort to teach her to drive. As with so many other things, she did pretty well on the technical aspects of driving. She stayed in her lane, rigidly adhered to all traffic rules, and got herself and her sometimes slightly unnerved instructor from here to there. However, as soon as something unexpected came up, Liz became flustered and needed her dad to talk her through the situation. The problem is, there are millions of situations in a driver's lifetime, and no way to prepare Liz for each and every one that might crop up.

When it became obvious that Liz would not be able to handle driving, I worried about how we were going to tell her. When it came time to renew her learner's permit, Bob and I decided to let her go ahead and get the new permit and we would break the bad news sometime before she became eligible for a license. Bob thought that the stress of the driving experience was beginning to overcome the allure and Liz might just give it up as a bad idea on her own.

As it turned out, we didn't have to be the bad guys. The form Liz had to fill out for renewal of her learner's permit asked if she had had a seizure in the last nine months. She reported that she had, and that made her ineligible to operate a motor vehicle. Not only did I feel bad about Liz's disappointment, I felt really stupid! Her seizures were so mild and so short in duration and so well-controlled by medication, it hadn't occurred to me that they would interfere with her driving. I asked the neurologist about it the next time Liz saw him and he said he had a photo sent to him by a patient who had seizures which were so mild and short in duration that she thought they would not interfere with her driving. The picture was of her car plowed into the side of a house.

Thankfully, a teen mentoring program called Just Friends came along just as Liz reached driving age. Unfortunately, teens who don't drive don't get to spend time away from their parents nearly often enough. Just Friends provided Liz with friends her age who drove her places. If they didn't drive, they hung out with her at the mall and movies where her dad or I dropped them off.

Liz had a few friends through this program, but Rose was, by far, the most special to Liz.

In Liz's words . . .

What I did with Just Friends, which it's a teen mentoring program where teens with disabilities are matched to a teen without a disability, which is the mentor and they engage their friendship doing one on one things a couple times a month, and once a week by calls. They also attended group events with all the other mentors and their friends once a month I think. Some group events they all did was hayrack ride, River City Roundup, and other group events scheduled.

Rose M. was my mentor when I was 17. I was matched to her, and she was a great mentor to me the last 16 years I've known her. She and I did weekly calls, went out on weekends to lunch, see a movie, walk on the bike trail, get ice cream, go over to Rose's and watch a movie, play pool, and any other one on one plans we thought of to do. Most of the time I did one on one plans with her, her mom, Irene came along, and it was always fun.

I have learned an experience of being matched to a mentor because of my disability, and the difference Rosie has made in my life, for all the fun things we have done over the years. You really learn a new experience, that you wouldn't have learned otherwise. She lives in Boston now, and her mom lives in Wyoming in Jackson. Even though they have moved from me, they have given and give me notice when they have been, and are coming to town, to schedule plans to lunch, or walk on the bike trail, or something planned when they're here to get a chance to see each other. We also correspond emails, long distance calls, Facebook, and cards or gifts shipped in the mail for birthdays and holidays of other ways we still stay in contact.

Just Friends not only gave Liz an outlet for her typical teen-aged disdain for all things parental, it went a long way toward teaching her how to be a friend. I think a common misconception about people on the autism spectrum is that they are all withdrawn and live in their own world without a need for interaction with others. For Liz this could not be further from the truth. She values and nurtures her friendships more than anyone I know. She spends hours visiting people in the neighborhood and much of the rest of her off-work time keeping in touch with friends and family through Facebook, emails, and phone calls. Liz's emails are legendary. Sometimes someone will share with me a particularly delightful or informative or touching email that Liz sent them. The one below is a great example of how incredibly detailed any correspondence from her can be. It is also a good illustration of the almost complete lack of white space in her emails. David says if you hold your head at just the right angle and stare with your eyes half closed, you can see a sailboat!

Duff and Barb,
My conference was great on the 11th through the 13th in Kearney, Nebraska, and I went down on the 11th and it was great. I went swimming at the Holiday Inn where I stayed, and it was great, and to dinner. Saturday was presentations all day, and I went to one on autism, which falls into what I have, as you know and it was interesting. Saturday night was the banquet, and music and dancing the rest of the night, and I went swimming for part of the night also, and it was great. Sunday, was the meeting on chapter reports and bylaws. The chapter reports were read by all cities of Nebraska, and I read the chapter report for Omaha. The bylaws were read, and will see if they pass or will be passed also, as bylaws is a huge thing whether they will pass, or have passed when it comes to whether they pass, or haven't passed, or didn't pass, and I know how bylaws are about passing, or didn't pass, as bylaws make a huge difference on passing. The presentation that was to be given on personal stories and a video what self advocacy means, wasn't presented, since no one was prepared to give it, and most of the year my self advocacy group worked on this video and personal stories what self advocacy means to present it, and I don't know it will be presented at another conference when everyone is more prepared and has more time to get it all together to present, or

if we'll try and have an inservice training on this, and see what happens, and will see if an inservice training happens, and what happens with this presentation that didn't get presented if it even will, or at an inservice training, and will see what happens with it. If there is an inservice training, I'll see what will be happening at it, or what is being done there at it. I came back Sunday afternoon the 13th, and it was great.Otherwise working, bowling weekly, mentoring with Creighton college buddies, Honey Sunday on and after November 3, and if you would like one or more, let me know, and I'll get yours to you over the holiday, when I get everyone else's to them, Creighton games into November, six Wednesdays away from seeing neurology, and see if I get off the Phenobarbetal, Wednesday, December 4, which is the Wednesday after Thanksgiving and the first Wednesday of December I see neurology, and all other things happening as always! Andy's school plans have changed recently I heard. School didn't work too well for Andy because of the brain injury [the result of complications from Meningitis] and short term memory, and it's too hard for him, in some parts of the brain that can't function on studying, and he's going to take a class at Metro, and he's going towards being a veterinarian's assistant, and will see how Metro works out for him. I told him that just because he had the brain injury from the illness that it doesn't mean he can't succeed and accomplish in anything, and he can succeed and accomplish things like I can the same, like me, and like everyone else. I told him to look at the things he succeeded and accomplished before and after the illness; before the illness he wrote great articles in the Reader paper that everyone thought were great articles, after the illness since it's been 8 $^{1/2}$ years, he tried school and it didn't work. Taking this class at Metro may work better for him, and I told him to keep trying, and to not give up, and you never know what you will succeed and accomplish, and he has accomplished and succeeded in more things than he thinks. I told him that just because I have autism and the language disorder of Pervasive Developmental Disorder, doesn't mean I can't accomplish and succeed in anything. I've served on boards, I have earned awards, I have read chapter reports, I have given presentations, I tried teaching nursing home residents at a nursing home how to use email and earned letters

from all over the United States when I earned my gold award when you were at my ceremony of it in 1998, I wrote essays for a book and had no idea I would have written a book, and it turns out I wrote a book, and all the things I have accomplished and succeeded and what I can succeed and accomplish, since I'm bright, smart, and intelligent like he is, and I know he can do the same like me and everyone else of keep trying and see what you succeed and accomplish, and he said I had some wise words to say, and will see how this other alternative works since school at Iowa Western didn't work that well for him.
Love your niece

All members of my family now sign our messages to each other with Liz's closing which, rather than expressing her affection, in her uniquely Lizzie way, demands the recipient's love. God I love this girl!

Not long ago, Liz got me back in touch with two cousins I hadn't seen in years. When I tried to explain to her why I had not gotten together with my cousins in such a long time, I could see my explanation was falling on deaf ears. In Liz's concrete thinking, if you're family and live in the same town, you see each other. Hmmm, I had a hard time seeing the error in her reasoning and invited everyone for dinner. We had a great time.

In Liz's words . . .

My friendship with my mom's cousin Liz is I discovered a connection through an important for safety article I had never seen before, that my friend Rose M. forwarded me, and I learned some helpful and useful tips and information about women's safety of being raped and their caution what to be aware of. Through the article, I discovered a connection with my friend Rose and my mom's cousin Liz. Liz and I correspond and have corresponded emails in the last 5 years since 2007 telling how things have been working, bowling, the convention, how my brothers, my mom and dad are, how Duff and Denny are of my mom's brothers of the O'Malley's of her first cousins and their kids. When Bill's [cousin Liz's husband] mom, dad, and brother died, Liz sent me emails which family member died, and I sent Bill sympathy cards for his mom's, dad's, and brother's deaths, that Bill greatly appreciated my thoughtfulness acknowledging sympathy in difficult times of loss. Bill has told me my letters are so thoughtful and personal, and leave him and Liz feeling lucky to have such a wonderful, loving person like Lizzy Sigler in their family. Liz and Bill are special to me, as I am special to them, and I love Liz and Bill more than anything and with affection, and Liz and Bill love me the same right back to me!

My friendship with Kathleen [mom's cousin] is I discovered her on Facebook. Kath moved back this summer, and she takes and has taken me bowling since she moved back here, and it's been great fun!

I also even broke an even 200 game, and close to 200 games with Kath, on September 9, 2012, and it was incredibly great, and I couldn't believe it! When Kath gets moved into her apartment, she and I are going to have slumber parties, and come over and see Liz and Bill often, which would be great fun! I have Kath's birthday card saved she sent me on my 33rd birthday on December 5, 2011, and it will always be saved with all the cards and notes Liz and Bill send and have sent me, and I won't throw it or any other cards or notes Kath sends and has sent me also, as special as I am to Kath as I am to Liz and Bill, and how special Kath is to me, and as special Liz and Bill are to me. I love Kath the same as I love Liz and Bill, and she loves me the same also. Liz and Bill and Kath are lucky and fortunate to have a special, thoughtful, and much loved friend, and first cousin once removed in their family, and to see often and make plans, and to have fun and a great time, and especially celebrating breaking 200 every time it gets broken in bowling! Our friendship won't ever be taken, and it will never be broken either!

Liz has developed another special friendship with my friend's daughter, Melanie.

In Liz's words . . .

My friendship with Melanie, an adult about three years younger than me that has cerebral palsy, has made a difference in her life and mine. She has a sense of humor, she loves to hear stories of any kind that have happened, any conversation being made asking how her summer was, work, her sister and brother, antwo nieces she has, and about anything. I set plans with her when I have time around working, social activities, bowling, seeing Creighton play in the winter, and everything on my schedule, to see a movie, go bowling, or come over to her place and play Wii. My friendship with her, I've realized the difference I made in her life, to someone that is handicapped and is in a wheelchair, and will never be able to walk, and I help out in several ways of pushing her in the wheelchair where she needs to be, or to offer to push her, I am a door holder at places to hold it open for someone to push her wheelchair through the door, and found I'm very helpful. She and I have a lot of fun together in the plans we've done, and plans we plan for the future also, and she's truly a lot of fun.

When she turned 18, Liz joined Best Buddies, a program founded by Anthony Shriver and, in Omaha, is affiliated with Creighton University

In Liz's words. . .

Best Buddies is similar to the Just Friends program, only adults 18 and older with disabilities are matched to Creighton students. The Creighton students are the college buddies, and the adult with a disability is their buddy. From October through April, there is one group event a month, usually a 2 hour event one Sunday a month. Most of the time, they're day events because college students have classes, and studying to do in the evening. Some of the group events all buddies and college buddies do once a month are bowling, Creighton baseball game, Creighton basketball game, the zoo, saw a tour of the new stadium at Ameritrade, and other different types of group events once a month over the years I've been involved in Best Buddies. The one on one plans the college buddy and their buddy can plan is, play basketball at the Kiewit Fitness Center at Creighton, come see their college buddy's dorm, see a movie, go to lunch or dinner, get dessert, have the college buddy come to their buddy's place and play games, play Wii, watch a movie, go out for a walk, or other kinds of one on one plans the college buddy and their buddy can plan for. It's a lot of fun hanging out with college kids.

I have learned also college buddies have made a difference in my life for their time and commitment they've put in. Even after my college buddy has graduated from Creighton, we always will still be friends, and stay in contact long distance, emails, trips made in town, and Facebook as well, as we did when they were in college at Creighton.

Once a year, Liz attends the annual People First of Nebraska Convention. This year was a special one for her. She was given the Ray Loomis Advocate of the Year award for her involvement in advocating for people with developmental disabilities. Receiving the award was an honor, but I think being a participant in the panel discussion of the movie, "The Music Within" was more important to Liz. Ever since that presentation, she has been on a mission to ensure that everyone in the Western Hemisphere sees the movie. God bless our friends and family who have agreed (sometimes been hounded into agreeing), to sit with Liz and watch. Fortunately, in addition to raising awareness of obstacles faced by people with disabilities, this is a good movie!

In Liz's words . . .

The convention is always a fun weekend. Everyone comes to the convention every year from Omaha, Lincoln, York, Grand Island,

Kearney, Norfolk, and other cities of Nebraska. People First of Nebraska is a self-advocacy organization. At the convention, people attend presentations all weekend on Saturday and Sunday morning, swimming at the pool at the Holiday Inn where everyone stays at. There's also the bake sale, t-shirt sales, the banquet on Saturday night, music and dancing the rest of the night after the banquet until midnight, and other fun things at the convention all weekend. Everyone sees the others that attend the convention from the other cities of Nebraska every year, and it's always fun to get to see everyone.

There was also a presentation given by me and 5 others on "The Music Within" movie. The movie is inspired by Richard Pimentel, an Army veteran who lost his hearing to a bomb blast while serving in Vietnam. While dealing with this new-found disability on his return to civilian life, Richard discovers that he can make a difference.

The six of us presented this on Saturday, October 10, 2009, from 1:00-4:00 in the afternoon. All six of us introduced ourselves before presenting, and when it came to your script to present, you read your part. It was presented in a room full of people, and everyone thought the presenters did great at presenting when it was through. I have also watched the DVD with other friends and family of mine that hadn't seen it yet and

121

I've been given compliments about what a great job presenting, and what a great movie it was, and that they enjoyed it.

The Hard Parts

I have been taught that an integral part of memoir writing is "facing the dragon," meaning you talk about the bad stuff. So I guess now it is time to talk about the hardest parts of being Liz's mother.

Hands down the hardest thing has been the rages. A few years ago, I was comparing notes about Liz with the president of a state autism society. She had a son whose diagnosis fell somewhere along the autism spectrum. As we visited, I remarked on how much our children had in common. The woman asked, "Does your daughter have rages?" I allowed as how Liz did indeed have pretty impressive episodes of out-of-control anger. They started when she was a little girl and occurred more and more frequently as she got older.

I mentioned that, as a baby, Lizzie hated being dressed. It wasn't just the handling that bothered her. Sometimes it was the feel of the clothing itself. Shortly after she began to walk, I got her up one morning and dressed her in a darling little handmade sundress that her Nana had gotten at one of those expensive grandma boutiques. When I stood her up, she erupted. She ran around the room howling and pulling at the dress until she tore it off. I never told her Nana.

One afternoon during Lizzie's To Kill a Mockingbirdathon, her brother, Andy, thought it was not entirely unreasonable for him to be permitted to watch something of his choice on the TV. Andy was young and still thought he could change Lizzie's mind with rational discourse. It was not the first, and certainly not the last, time Lizzie would disabuse him of this notion. He went into the family room, announced that since Lizzie had watched the movie 13 times by then, it was his turn to watch, and changed the channel. Liz went ballistic and chaos ensued. By the time I pulled them apart, both of Andy's forearms were covered with scratch marks where Lizzie had raked her fingernails down them.

I remember another incident when Lizzie was five, this one at our neighborhood swimming pool. Most of the families on our block went to the pool almost every day in the summer. On this day, as we mothers visited, always keeping one eye on our kids, I noticed David headed toward the boys' locker room, followed closely by his little sister. I lept out of my lawn chair, flew across the pool deck and caught Lizzie just before she reached the entrance. I told her she wasn't allowed in the boys' locker room and tried to explain why. The logic of separate facilities for boys and girls eluded her and she had a tantrum of monumental proportions. While that normally wouldn't have drawn too much attention from a two year old, seeing a mother physically restraining a child Lizzie's age as she screamed and flailed about, captured the interest of most of the people within hearing. As Lizzie shrieked and people stared, a local TV personality, who was at the pool with his kids, came over and asked if he could help. I think I convinced him that I wasn't abusing my child, just trying to get her to see reason, but this was another time that being Liz's mom put me in danger of seeing myself on the six o'clock news.

As she got older, Liz's anger reached fever pitch so often and in response to such small provocation, that the rest of us in the family walked on eggshells a lot of the time. Most of the wrath seemed to surface when we asked her a question. The question didn't have to be particularly intrusive. For her, just being asked something – anything - was an intrusion. "Is tomorrow trash day?" could spark a knock-down drag out as easily as, "What's *your* problem?" The typical pattern was that someone in the family would ask Liz a question, she would come back with a nasty, snotty reply, we would retort with hurt feelings or irritation and then it was game on. Some of these altercations lasted for hours and some for days.

One snowy winter day when Liz was about 12 years old, she was outside shoveling with her dad. Suddenly, the rhythmic scraping of the shovels was interrupted by a string of curse words that would make a sailor blush. To my amazement they were coming from Liz! Liz doesn't curse (a quality of hers I try unsuccessfully to emulate). From that day to this I have rarely heard her use the word "damn." But on that day, she was furiously yelling at Bob about something and peppering her accusations with big time profanities. I was shocked and terrified the neighbors would hear and got her to come inside to tell me what was wrong. She told me her dad was trying to tell her what shovel to use. That was all it took. She was so incensed at him, and now me as I tried to reason with her, that I was seriously afraid she was going to hit me. I don't remember what it took to calm her down that day, but I never heard her talk like that again.

For many, many years, when Liz got in the car or came in the front door and I said, "Hi." My greeting, if it were acknowledged at all, would be returned with a barely audible grunt. I handled this issue in a couple of completely ineffective ways. I either let Liz get away with the rude behavior or I demanded a response, telling her how bad her manners were. Ignoring her was the cause of festering resentment for me. Forcing her to answer always brought on a battle royal. She would tell me that she always said, "Hi," that I always got mad at her for nothing, that I just thought she was a rude girl who never said anything nice, and on and on and on. She often screamed that I was sorry I had her for a daughter. I told her that she was wrong and I had never said or thought that I didn't want her for a daughter. I just wanted her to use good manners and act like I existed. She said she did use good manners and it was stupid to say that she acted like I wasn't there. How could she act like I wasn't there when it was obvious I was there? It was usually at this point that I withdrew, exhausted, unable to dispute her logic.

A sure-fire way to start one of these anger fests was to ask Liz where she had been or what she had been doing after she had been away from the house for hours. By the time I remembered that asking her such a question was an insult to her, it was too late. Her reaction went from zero to wrath in 60 seconds. I would meet her resentment with my own and we were off and running. I wasn't able to convince her that I might have asked the same question of anyone, that I was merely curious and trying to have a conversation. She said that I wouldn't ask David or Andy where they went and I don't tell her where I go every time I leave the house so why should she have to tell me? I told her that she didn't have to, I was just curious and I certainly wouldn't be insulted if she asked me where I had been. After an hour of responding to her in every way I could think of from rational patience to pissy self-righteousness, the emotions had escalated to a frightening level. I tried to move on by telling Liz I didn't want to talk about it anymore and we should just drop it. I knew that wouldn't stop her, but I was exhausted so I just quit talking, went into my bedroom and locked the door before one of us resorted to physical violence. Liz stood outside and shouted 78 times (I counted), "You wish you never had me!"

Once the fury set in (mine included), there was no reasoning with her or outlasting her. She flew into a frenzy of accusations about how she didn't do anything and I just wanted to be mad at her for nothing and I thought she was the rudest person I knew and I wished she weren't my daughter. I responded in kind, yelling and spewing accusations. She *was* rude and she didn't care how other people felt and she always had to be right and get the last word. These fights went on for years, getting worse all the time. It got to the point where, rather than chance a blow-up, I barely spoke to my daughter.

Things had gotten so bad about five years ago, that I made an appointment for us with a counselor. We only went three times because Liz hated it and didn't see the point. I have read that talk therapy isn't effective for people on the autism spectrum, and I had promised her that I wouldn't put her through it once a week if she hated it, so we quit. Luckily, before we did, I got one of the most valuable pieces of advice I have ever had. When I described our marathon battles and Liz's irrational response to anything I said, the counselor's comment was, "You're turning this into a power struggle. Just back down instead of trying to prove to her how she is wrong." I asked what I should do if she looked at a black car and said it was white, the kind of thing that could easily happen when we were locked in combat. He told me to agree with her and let it go, then revisit the subject the next day when emotions weren't running so high. It wasn't long before I had an opportunity to try his suggestion and the result was incredible. The next time Liz said some off the wall thing that couldn't possibly be true, I calmly told her she was right and that was the end of it. The next day we talked it over and I explained why I was angry and we were actually able to have a discussion about our feelings – miraculous!

Removing the rage factor has allowed me to get some insight into what seems to me to be Liz's lack of appropriate emotional reactions to some situations. Recently she was asked to spend a few hours with her friend Melanie while her mom was at the doctor. The time she was needed conflicted with a basketball game and it took a lot of talking to convince Liz to do the favor and not tell Melanie or her mom or dad that she really wasn't crazy about the idea. She was nice to Melanie and didn't gripe about the imposition, but when I thanked her afterwards her comment was, "Even though I didn't want to be counted on." In bygone days, that was the kind of remark that would send me into a tizzy. Wiser now, I let it go, but later, as I got to thinking about it, I mentioned to Liz that even though she had done the favor, she hadn't been very gracious about it. She objected, reminding me that she hadn't said anything rude to Melanie or her parents even though she didn't want to miss the game. I told her that we all do things we don't particularly want to do, but didn't she at least like the good feeling she got when she helped a friend. She immediately got teary – always an indication that she doesn't understand what I am talking about. It occurred to me that she doesn't get that feeling! I now believe she should get double credit for doing favors, since the only reason she has for doing them is because she is supposed to. I gave Liz triple credit when, a few days later she said she would sit with Mel whenever she was needed. She will never stop surprising me.

Even though I tried to follow the counselor's advice, there were still times when Liz and I lost it. A few years ago Liz and I went out to dinner with my friend, Robin. Liz got dessert and I asked her if I could have a bite. She responded in a nasty way and I backed off knowing what kind of a scene could ensue if I pushed. Robin, however, was having none of it. To my horror she said, "Liz, I can't sit here and allow you to speak to your mother in such a rude way." Liz immediately burst into tears. Now Liz bursting into tears is no small thing. She sobbed so loudly I swear a couple of other customers were dialing 911. My friend took Liz to the bathroom thinking she would be able to calm her down. I knew better. In about 10 minutes my friend signaled to me that they were going to the car and she left with a distraught Liz in tow. I followed behind with a look that I hope conveyed to the other diners my sympathy for the woman ahead of me who had so upset her daughter. I walked to the end of the parking lot farthest away from her car so no one would think I was connected to them in any way. They picked me up on the way out, Liz still sobbing desperately.

As soon as we walked in the house, Liz went straight to her room. I didn't see her again until the next day when she came to me angrily explaining what I had done wrong. That did it! I had had 30 years of this and it was beginning to make me a little cranky. I told her that I didn't care how she felt I only cared how I felt and I felt bad. She had embarrassed me by speaking so rudely to me in front of all those people and I wanted an apology. I told her this wasn't about her feelings it was about mine. At one point I said, "I don't care if you have a disability or 10 disabilities, the way you act affects other people and you hurt my feelings!" For three days, she bombarding me with the by now familiar litany – "You wish I weren't your daughter." "You just don't want to talk to me." "You always say I'm rude," etc., etc., but I held my ground. On the third night, I was lying in bed watching TV. Liz came into my room and lay down, put her head on my lap, apologized and sobbed for a half hour. I will never know what got through to her, but from that day to this we have not had another battle. For sure we have had some arguments, but just the regular kind. Liz seems to be a much happier person. Most of the time she is friendly and cheerful and pleasant to be around. I am not sure where her anger went, but a years-long pattern was broken and I feel like the sun has been shining on us ever since that day. I told Robin that just maybe the only reason she was put on this earth was to bring about this astonishing change in my relationship with my daughter. As far as I was concerned it was enough. I don't think Robin wholly agreed with that, but she was mighty proud that the Disaster at the Red Lobster ended so well.

Ever since that night, Liz says hello when she comes in the house, she thanks me when I give her a ride somewhere, she tells me to have a good day when I drop her at work. Granted, I always initiate the exchanges, but these days, Liz always responds. My day-to-day interactions with her have improved so dramatically that I scarcely remember when the dragon lurked around every innocuous question I might ask. I am relieved every day that the battles are over.

Of course the constant state of negative emotion took its toll on the rest of the family as well as on Liz and me. Her relationships with her brothers took so many hits over the years that they drew away from her. Even today, when Liz is almost a different person, it still seems hard for them to talk to her. And why not, when they tried a hundred times over to include her in a conversation and were met with a surly reply? I hope as they see that the new Liz is here to stay, they will be able to get past old rejections and forge new relationships with her – and that she will be able to respond in kind.

I was surprised to learn that this part of our life made a bit more of an impression on me than on Liz. After laboring for hours to find the right words to describe these turbulent times in an honest and forthright way; admitting my own anger and loss of control; taking my share of the blame; castigating myself for not seeking help earlier, I asked Liz how she felt about the fights. She said, "What fights?"

Placing a close second behind the anger, is the fear I feel when I think about Liz's vulnerability to the million-and-one things that could, but probably won't, happen. I don't think I'll ever be completely at ease when she is out and about in the world. Over the years, I have managed to put my apprehension on the back burner, but I am only truly comfortable when she is safe at home. She takes the bus to and from her summer job downtown and walks to and from her job at the university. Sometimes she stops to run an errand or get a bite after work. If she doesn't show up when I think she should, I am sure she has been (a) kidnapped, (b) mortally injured crossing the street, (c) assaulted by all manner of evil doers, and\or (d) drowned in the Missouri River, which is a full 10 miles away from any point on her route. I want to ask where she has been, but, as she has pointed out at varying decibel levels, it is not really any of my business. She is, after all, an adult.

The only rule I enforce without fail is that she must be home, or at least back on our block, before dark. She is 34 years old and I still hold my breath if she isn't inside the house the moment the sun sets. This caused one of our epic brouhahas a few years ago. I tried to explain the dangers of a woman being out alone after dark. Liz's theory was that, since none of my dire predictions about her safety had as yet come to pass, they never would. Obviously she was doing something right and I was an alarmist, and not a very bright one at that. I dug in my heels on this one and would not be moved. Liz could see this, though she would suffer the rack before she admitted I was right. I won that battle and she has returned home before dark every night since.

Another particularly worrisome thing is sex. In order to protect Liz's dignity, I won't expound on this topic too much, but, like any mother, I worry. When I approached her about protection, just in case, she told me that she had discussed this with her doctor, and they had decided it wasn't necessary at this point. I wanted to say, "What about the monsters hanging around every corner waiting specifically for you?" I didn't say that because it would just reinforce Liz's opinion that I am a paranoid worry wart with a catastrophic outlook on life. She seems to be well aware of the dangers of predators as evidenced by the fact that she sent an article on how to guard against sexual assault to most of the women and some of the men on her email list. She seems to be handling this area of her life, so I back off. I fret, but I think not much more than any mother. Well that's a lie, but let's just say the anxiety is manageable.

A noted disability advocate, Robert Perske, wrote in an article titled, "The Dignity of Risk and the Mentally Retarded," that to deny people with intellectual disabilities their share of risk experiences is to rob them of a certain dignity. While I agree with this in theory, after 30 some years of holding my breath, I want to say, "You try it, Bob!"

My biggest fear is what will happen to Liz when her dad and I die, a concern that she shares with me. While she is 99% independent and can handle most things in her life, she would not be able to live without support. It is not because she isn't capable of getting herself back and forth to work or doing her laundry as long as those procedures stay the same. But there are a million "what ifs" in daily life. Most of us can adapt to them when they actually happen. For Liz, things outside her routine are a big problem. If she would lose her job and have to look for a new one, if the washer would break and have to be repaired or replaced, if the bus didn't go to where her work is, she would need someone to interpret the new situation for her, to tell her what she needs to do and make sure she understands everything she has been told. She asked me once, "If we go down to the basement when there is a tornado, why don't we go down to the basement if the house is on fire?" So now, whenever I consider Bob and me being gone together for any length of time, like say, eternity, I immediately picture Liz sitting in the basement as the house burns down above her.

For Liz preparing meals would be a big problem. I have sporadically tried to teach her to cook, but the recipes are complicated, the utensils are confusing and the marks on the measuring cups are hard to see. And not just for me. Having admitted my failure as a culinary coach, I tried to redeem myself by driving her back and forth to cooking classes and by hiring college students to cook with her. These efforts have resulted in a three-ring binder stuffed full of recipes, but Liz can't follow them without help.

I thought we were lucky to be living in the age of the microwave. I figured she could just zap something for dinner and supplement her diet with salads, veggies and dip, and bananas. Have you ever read the directions on a microwave meal? "Microwave on high for two minutes. Slit the plastic over the apple pan dowdy, turn the plate one quarter to the right, heat for one more minute at 75% power. Let stand for two minutes while you take three umbrella steps away from the oven." When I go out of town or out to dinner I give Liz one step instructions on how to reheat frozen soups or leftovers that I have ready for such occasions. Inevitably, the meals are untouched. We live within spitting up distance of many fast food restaurants, so when I am gone, Liz usually eats fast food, while the nutritious meals stay safely tucked away in the freezer. Neither her heart nor her pocket book would survive this lifestyle for long if she had to do it every night.

People ask if Liz can't just move into a group home. There are a few problems with that plan. She functions at such a high level and is so independent that to move from a life in which she decides what she will do day-to-day to a home that is governed by rules imposed on her by others would be intolerable for Liz.

Even if she were a candidate for a group home, the last time I checked there were upwards of 2,000 people in Nebraska waiting for a slot to open. And, even if there were a suitable placement available for Liz, she would have to qualify under certain guidelines. One would think that someone with Liz's diagnoses and history would be a shoe-in, but that ain't necessarily so. When she applied for Supplemental Security Income right after she left school, someone in the state Social Security office who had never laid eyes on Liz determined that she did not have a disability, this in spite of the fact that she had spent 18 years receiving special education services and had reams of paper full of test results verifying her disability eight ways to Sunday.

We had a similar experience when Andy got bacterial meningitis and a sinus infection that invaded his braincausing many strokes and respiratory arrest. His neurosurgeon said he might as well have gone through a windshield of a car and was lucky to have survived, albeit with permanent neurological damage. When he applied for SSI and short term Social Security Disability Insurance, the state denied his claim, which was in effect saying that he was fine and perfectly able to go right back to a full time job immediately after a 30 day hospital stay. In my experiences with my family, the safety net in our state for people who need government support is so full of holes that I am not sure who it is catching.

Liz will probably live with, or at least in close proximity, to one of her brothers when we are gone, please God in the far, far distant future. This is not what I want. Her brothers and her sister-in-law have assured us that they will be there when they are needed (that's another thing we do in our family) and make sure Liz is taken care of. The problem with that solution is that we don't know where they will be living or what their circumstances will be when the time comes. The idea of Liz having to be completely uprooted or becoming a burden to her siblings keeps me awake many nights. It makes me feel guilty that I might have to transfer my responsibility over to my sons. It feels like, if I have not designed an independent life plan for Liz by the time I die, I have not done my job.

And what if she doesn't have brothers by the time we're gone? Talk about staying awake at night! I think if you asked most parents of children with disabilities, regardless of the child's age, what their greatest hope is, they would say that they live five minutes longer than their child. Hoping that your child dies before you might seem macabre, but picturing the alternative is worse.

Still I haven't given up. I know that the perfect roommate for Liz is out there somewhere and that between Bob and me, the hopefully soon-to-be-named roommate's family, and the state Developmental Disabilities office, we will be able to put together a package of support that will allow Liz the dignity that should be her right. Contrary to what some people think, Liz and people like her don't want to be dependent. They are tax-paying citizens of this country and they deserve a leg up if that is what it takes to give them lives of independence and self-respect.

So What's it Really Like?

Some people have said that when you have a child with a disability, you experience a kind of death – the death of the child you thought you were going to have and the death of the dreams you had for that child. There have been times when I have felt that way. When I celebrate with other mothers their daughters' milestones, I am thrilled for them. But I can't help thinking about what I have missed. I never got to see Liz in a school play. I never got to wave her off on her first date. I never got to see her accept that Ivy League diploma or walk down the aisle at her wedding or hold her baby in her arms. The ache I feel over those disappointments will never go away.

Even though I have grieved the loss of the proud moments I thought I was going to have, I have had moments of great joy. I have seen my daughter take a bus to work and back on her own. I have seen her call her doctor and make an appointment. I have seen her read a newspaper article over and over until she finally makes some sense of it. I have seen her walk two miles to the drugstore and back to get her prescription filled so she doesn't have to be dependent on me for a ride. I have seen her searching for the right question to ask someone to show that she is interested in them. I have seen her balance her checkbook. Even though these moments are not the ones I had pictured in my mother-daughter dreams, they make my heart swell.

I think the loss I feel most deeply comes from Liz's difficulty expressing, and maybe even feeling, affection. She often draws away or submits awkwardly when I try to hug her. I don't remember that she ever initiated a hug with me. She writes about loving people, and I believe she feels an emotion she calls love, but I am not sure what that means for her. My daughter hasn't said the words, "I love you" to me out loud since she was a little girl and it was part of the bedtime tucking-in ritual. I know it isn't because she doesn't love me in her way. I know it isn't because she withholds her love on purpose. I know that her particular disability makes it difficult if not impossible for her to experience certain emotions, much less express them. But that doesn't stop me imagining what it might be like for her to say, "I love you, Mom." Maybe some day.

Worth Keeping

The best description I have ever read about what it is like to have a child who has a disability is the famous essay by Emily Perl Kingsley, "Welcome to Holland."

I am often asked to describe the experience of raising a child with a disability - to try to help people who have not shared that unique experience to understand it, to imagine how it would feel. It's like this......

When you're going to have a baby, it's like planning a fabulous vacation trip - to Italy. You buy a bunch of guide books and make your wonderful plans. The Coliseum. The Michelangelo David. The gondolas in Venice. You may learn some handy phrases in Italian. It's all very exciting.

After months of eager anticipation, the day finally arrives. You pack your bags and off you go. Several hours later, the plane lands. The stewardess comes in and says, "Welcome to Holland."

"Holland?!?" you say. "What do you mean Holland?? I signed up for Italy! I'm supposed to be in Italy. All my life I've dreamed of going to Italy."

But there's been a change in the flight plan. They've landed in Holland and there you must stay.

The important thing is that they haven't taken you to a horrible, disgusting, filthy place, full of pestilence, famine and disease. It's just a different place.

So you must go out and buy new guide books. And you must learn a whole new language. And you will meet a whole new group of people you would never have met.

It's just a different place. It's slower-paced than Italy, less flashy than Italy. But after you've been there for a while and you catch your breath, you look around.... and you begin to notice that Holland has windmills....and Holland has tulips. Holland even has Rembrandts.

But everyone you know is busy coming and going from Italy... and they're all bragging about what a wonderful time they had there. And for the rest of your life, you will say "Yes, that's where I was supposed to go. That's what I had planned."

And the pain of that will never, ever, ever, ever go away... because the loss of that dream is a very very significant loss.

But... if you spend your life mourning the fact that you didn't get to Italy, you may never be free to enjoy the very special, the very lovely things ... about Holland.

Sometimes I think Liz was lucky to draw me for her mother. After all, I have a lot of experience in special education and disability issues. I have many resources that have enabled me to help her more than I ever could have without that knowledge. I am a pretty good advocate. Most of the time, though, I can't imagine why I was picked to be the mother of this remarkable woman. When I snap at Liz because she is not getting what I say, when my eyes glaze over as she gives me the 10-minute bowling report, when I hurt her feelings by showing my impatience, I am utterly convinced that she would be better off with anyone but me and I want to stab myself in the eye.

Shameless as it is, I went fishing for compliments, and asked Liz to write something about what it was like to have me for a mother. I couldn't have asked for a better report card. Maybe I'm doing okay after all.

In Liz's words. . .

I'm grateful, thankful, feel fortunate, and lucky to have the mom I have and have had all through my lifetime. She has gotten me through school, and after frustration in 8th grade, of not learning anything, she changed me over to special education school at Madonna School, that gives kids with learning problems/learning disabilities the ability to learn. Kids go to school there and move on to adult life of working, and their experiences and accomplishments they succeed!

My mom has also helped me find employment after school completion, where to look for employment at, and seeking for ideas what to do for employment I'm capable of, and I learned from her what discrimination is.

The Ollie Webb story tape is very interesting about Ollie Webb's life, but also interesting with my mom's speech telling about what the organization does, and the information provided to parents to get their child through their adult years, and her speech is incredibly great and helpful!

My mom is also forgetful as she tells me, and she uses and has used me for reminders believe it or not, what to get at home, the store, errands, whatever it is she can't and won't remember herself, as she knows I can remember things without reminders given to myself.

She also is a lot of fun, talkative, helpful, she loves going places with me, as well as I like going with her places to shopping which is one of my favorite things to do of always keep buying more jewelry of earrings, rings, and watches, going to lunch or dinner somewhere, plays, movies, trips, and plans and places she and I went and go to over the years.

She's helpful in dropping me off at work as a favor or when the weather isn't great and getting me at work also if weather isn't great or just for a favor, she'll get me to places on time I have to be at I can't get to myself in time.

I always have my mom on my side, and I know she's always there for me in times of need, and I always talk to her about stressful and hard times, or times I feel I need to talk to someone, that I know I can always talk to her, and I know I can always count on her, and I'm never afraid to talk to her about anything, even if it isn't very often

Even though I know I can write, I had no idea I was going to be writing a book about all the experiences I've had in life, my involvements, my employments, school, my mom of the great mom she is and has been to me, and all the several things I can write and have written about already that has happened in my lifetime.

I don't know where I would be today if I didn't have the mom I have and have had all my life and all the great things she's done for me and continues to in her years of being a mom and motherhood to me, and I certainly couldn't ask for a better mom than her, she's the greatest and the best mom I could ever have and could ever ask for, I'll never forget her, I love her and love her more than anything, and I thank my mom for everything in her years of motherhood to me, and for her love and support!

I read a theory that before our souls come to earth, we are given the opportunity to choose to make the journey with someone else. I've thought about this at times, and I wonder whether, given the choice, I would choose to be Liz's mother. I know for sure I would not choose that she have a disability. The world is not tolerant of difference, so if the universal teacher were asking that I take that on voluntarily, I would surely have put my head down on my desk or stared out the window or asked permission to go to the lavatory like I did in school so I wouldn't be chosen. But if the question were put a different way, if someone had said, "I have a baby girl here, waiting to go down. She is going to have a lot of challenges in her life and she needs someone who is willing to make the trip with her," even knowing what I know now I would have shot my hand into the air and waved it around like that obnoxious kid in fifth grade, until the teacher saw me and made me Liz's buddy. And I wouldn't have regretted it for a minute. Because for all the moments of confusion and turmoil and doubt and anger and fear and self-pity I have felt as Elizabeth's mother, there have been experiences I would never have had otherwise, and I treasure those experiences. Seeing the world through Liz's eyes, to the extent that I can, has been fascinating. The things she says and the way she says them delight me all the time; sometimes they are purely hilarious. The joy I have been able to recognize over the small things, the kindness I have experienced from so many, many people, the feeling of purpose and overwhelming love that my daughter has brought to my life has made this an extraordinary journey. And it ain't over yet!

Appendix A

Tips for Parents

This is a grab bag of hints and suggestions for parents who have children with disabilities. It probably won't mean a lot to other people, so I put it at the end of the book. Readers should feel free to skip this section if you don't have a child with a disability. These bits of wisdom, in no particular order, are things that I, and some other parents, have learned as we raised our children, and we wanted to share them.

- I have learned an important lesson in dealing with all of the professionals in Liz's life. Sometimes, I made snap judgments, as in the case of Liz's neurologist and her sixth grade teacher. I decided that I didn't like them and they didn't have Liz's best interests at heart, which couldn't have been further from the truth. As parents you'll be dealing with many professionals. Always give them two chances to get on your good side – even if you're going through a bad patch. If they don't come around after that, you can kick them to the curb, but everybody deserves a second chance – except for that really mean swim teacher.

- Don't take yourself to the woodshed because you lose your patience sometimes. My clan, the O'Malleys, are not famous for their patience. When that virtue was passed out, we were probably in a pub wondering what you had to do to get a pint. I promise you your child will forgive you when you are having a less-than-parent-of-the-year day. Tomorrow will come and you'll do better - or, if not, there's always the next day.

- I have heard many people say how lucky some family is that they live in a certain school district or state because they get Early Intervention services for their baby for free. Please tell everyone you know that *every* local school district provides free services to infants and toddlers who have disabilities. No matter how young your little one is, if you think there might be a problem, call your school district office. They will help you locate the professionals who can help you.

- The earlier a family begins services, the better it is for the baby and family. Some doctors and neonatal staff at a hospital may not be aware of the early intervention services that are available through the schools. You would be doing them and the families they serve a huge favor by taking some brochures to local doctors' offices and hospitals.

- *Always* ask questions if you don't understand or agree with something. Sometimes professionals forget and use acronyms or catch phrases that families aren't familiar with. If that happens, stop them and ask them to clarify. They won't think you are ignorant and they will be happy to explain.

- (From Mary Ann) For parents of infants and toddlers – use the help of your Services Coordinator when transitioning from home based services to preschool. The Services Coordinator knows about your family and the services that your child is entitled to and can ask questions that you might not think of.

- (From Mary Ann) If you have a good relationship with your Services Coordinator invite her to the first IEP meeting so that she can give you a sense of security. Make sure everything you want for your child is written down in the IEP. For instance, if you want help with potty training or help teaching your child to tie her shoes, make sure that it is included.

- (From Mary Ann) What I have learned as K's mom is that in order to make things happen -- for school, her job, her activities, her annual reports to the court and to Social Security, etc. -- I had to be right on top of everything. If I did not do what I was supposed to do as her parent, things would not get done.

- Never be afraid to ask for more, make people accountable or compromise when it might be helpful. Your child deserves to have the same opportunities that any child has.

- K has a wonderful sense of humor and loves to make people laugh. She is good to have around when I am having a bad day. I have often said that if everyone in the world had a touch of Down syndrome it would certainly be a different place.

- (From Judy) Don't try to be a miracle worker. My daughter got a strep infection in the hospital the day after she was born which led to seizures, hemorrhages and cerebral palsy. When Melanie was one year old we had six standing therapy appointments per week plus keeping up with the recommendations and assignments from seven doctors. I was the perfect candidate for assignments. I was eager, capable and wanted to maximize my daughter's abilities. If I was failing at something I just stayed up later and worked harder -- I was in much denial, fed by the unknown and stories of mothers who made the difference in whether or not their child walked, talked, spoke or went to a regular school. I had to quit my job and we were very poor, and had medical bills in spite of our insurance. Finally, I had a breakdown. The therapy I got two years later saved me and my family. I had to learn that I couldn't do it all. I had to let some things go or I was going to lose my health, my marriage, my friends and the support of my other children. I learned that in a family where there is a child with a disability, everyone, including that child, has to give up something. I told the therapists Mel was a total child living in a family, even if they thought their particular therapy was more important than the others. My savior was my pediatrician who put things into order and gave me permission to not try to introduce the glasses and the braces at the same time, etc. He told me Melanie's brother and sister were going to start resenting her if I didn't give them some of my time and attention. I told him I was going to start lying to unreasonable doctors and therapists and in his big jolly voice he said: "GOOD!"

- If your child receives special education services, even if it is just speech, she has an IEP. If you don't have a copy of the IEP or you can't remember having a meeting, call your child's teacher and tell him you want to set up a meeting to clarify things. Find out what is on the IEP, who is responsible for providing the services and what success will look like.

- (From Judy) When Melanie went from preschool to grade school an I.E.P. meeting was held. Her teacher, three therapists, a school psychologist and a high ranking district representative were present along with my husband and me. They went around the table and each person told of the many things Melanie couldn't do. We had been asked to bring our wishes but it was clear the die was cast as to her placement for the next year. As the reports went on I started to cry -- no one noticed. They were there to convince me that Melanie was a child with multiple, severe disabilities and she needed a self-contained classroom. They had no idea that I was very open to that as the integrated kindergarten had left Melanie frustrated all the time. When it came to me, I said that I couldn't say anything because not only did I not have a choice but "You are in denial" was written like a neon sign on all of their faces. I just cried, signed the paper and took my beautiful little girl with so many abilities home to fight another day. The next year Melanie had a wonderful teacher (who by the way was warned about me and laughed about it later).We had a partnership and the IEP meetings changed. I ran the meetings. In the middle of the table was a picture of my truly beautiful, happy child. We started with three things that we could celebrate over the past six months. Then each person was required to suggest three things we as a team could work on. After that, recording the behavioral objectives could go on and I would sign anything, but they had to play my way first. It was amazing how the meetings changed and how much more we appreciated each other and Melanie!

- Be informed. Your role as parent is just as important as any other professional on the IEP team. By law your ideas and suggestions must carry just as much weight as any others when determining goals, objectives and related services. Even though you might not have an education or speech or medical background, you have a good idea of what other children are doing at your child's age in areas like language development, social interaction and behavior. Most importantly you know what you want for your child. Make a list of the things what you want him to accomplish and discuss them with the rest of the IEP team. Then, together, you can design some programs or strategies for helping him reach these goals.

- Often, the biggest bone of contention on an IEP is what related services will be provided by the school district. Parents need to know that the school district is only required to provide the related services that are *necessary for your child to reach the IEP goals*. Being informed puts you in a good position to negotiate and prevents you from digging in on things your child is not entitled to. The number of hours per day and days per month of a related service will be negotiated, but no school district representative or school board can say, "We aren't providing speech (or OT or transportation) this year." Any related service listed on your child's IEP must be provided or paid for by the school district. If you feel your child needs more or different related services than the school district will provide, ask the IEP team for suggestions about where you might be able to get the extra services and how you might pay for them.

- The school is *not* legally responsible for your child reaching every IEP goal. Once when I suggested to a teacher that we revise some of the goals he had set, he said, "Oh sure, and then when she doesn't meet them, you can sue me." He was wrong, but it is a common misconception. That was neither here nor there. At that point I wasn't interested so much in suing him as tossing a slushie in his face.

- Remember that the professionals who work with your child are people who, by an overwhelming majority, care about kids. The law is in place to protect your child against the professional or school district official who is more protective of his or her power or the school district's coffers than your child's rights.

- One of the things that made me crazy when I worked at the Parent Center was when I asked parents what their child's disability was and they didn't know. If your child has an IEP, her disability is included in one of the 11disability categories listed in the IDEA. Surprisingly, sometimes parents are not aware of this.

- People have argued for a long time about the disadvantages of labeling children. Some think the label puts limitations on expectations. Others feel that a label can never adequately describe a specific disability. That debate is ongoing. The one thing I know as a parent is that you need to have a label ready when it comes time to access services, both educational and adult. If you have evaluations with a specific label clearly spelled out and\or one with an IQ score or performance level, put them in a place where you can find them later. I have needed these labels and numbers when trying to access particular placements in the school setting, Supplemental Security Income, Vocational Rehabilitation services, and private insurance. In Liz's case, because her disability is not a visible one, having a label has gained her some sympathy from all those people who think she's fine and I'm crazy. At least it made them realize that someone besides me thinks she has some obstacles to overcome and also that some of her seemingly rude behaviors are not intentional.

- If you disagree with the school district's evaluation, you have the right to get an independent evaluation at the school district's expense. A word of caution, though. If you are thinking about getting an independent evaluation, you should contact the school district before you do it.

They will either agree to pay for the independent evaluation or ask that a hearing officer decide whether you are entitled to one at school district expense. If you go ahead with outside testing and the hearing officer denies your request for payment, you will have to pay out of your own pocket.

- Go over the results of the three-year reevaluations carefully. Ask whether there have been significant changes in your child's level of functioning in any areas. Ask the multidisciplinary team if they think any goals or objectives should be modified as a result of these changes. If you don't ask these questions, some goals that should be dropped will stay on the IEP and newer, more practical goals might never be added. Also make sure the goals are realistic for your child. My friend's daughter had an occupational therapy goal to zip her pants. This woman has cerebral palsy and cannot stand without holding on to something. Realizing that zipping up pants would be impossible for her, her mother has always bought pull on slacks for her, rendering this goal not only unnecessary but ludicrous!

- The law says that children with disabilities should be educated with typical children "to the maximum extent appropriate." This is my particular high horse, but I don't think "to the maximum extent appropriate" necessarily means to the maximum extent possible. For some children, like Liz, less was more. She was not capable of reaching her potential by spending most, much less all, of her time in the regular classroom or, for that matter, in a regular school.

- Know what rights you and your child have under special education law. There is at least one Parent Center in every state. They all present workshops on parents' rights, as do school districts, advocacy groups, disability lawyers, etc. The point of the law is not to create an adversarial relationship between you and the school district. It is to ensure that you, as your child's most important advocate, have the same knowledge as the professionals who work with her. This creates teamwork that makes it possible to create the best programs.

- Adult social programs are a huge part of Liz's life. Check with Parent Centers, Arcs, and other disability support groups in your area to find out what social opportunities, Special Olympic Sports teams, buddy programs, classes, etc. are available. Then be prepared to spend lots of time in the car! Liz has a more active social life than I do.

- Don't expect that there will be a magic moment when you adjust, once and for all, to the fact that your child has a disability. The shock and sadness diminish and there will be long periods of time when you can speak about your child with joy and happiness and humor. And then, usually at an inopportune moment, someone will ask an innocent question or you will see someone your child's age and the reality that you thought you had come to terms with months or years ago hits you as if you were hearing the news for the first time. You may be at a family gathering and get a little teary; you might be at a movie and find yourself blubbering so loudly that people turn to see what's up (for me it was "The Other Sister"); you might be like the well-known speaker I heard addressing several hundred people at a national convention, who choked up when she mentioned her 40 year old "child." She quickly recovered and said, "Wow! That hasn't happened in a long time!" Don't worry about it or beat yourself up because you think you should be over it by now. You'll never be over it, but, believe it or not, "it" won't always be the first thing you think about when you wake up in the morning.

- Find some support from other parents. No one could ask for better support than I have gotten from family and friends (mine and Liz's), but no one except another parent who has a child like yours can truly understand what it is like. I urge you to call someone. Another parent can help you through a bad day and celebrate with you when the good stuff happens. Call any or all of the PTIs, disability support groups, the public school system, and advocacy groups near you and ask if they have or know of any parent support groups in your area.

- (From Judy) Late in the game for me I had a wonderful opportunity that I wish I could have had earlier. At a day-long parent conference, we broke up into disability-specific groups. I had never had the chance to be with people whose main concerns, like mine, were orthopedic issues. I got to ask the tough questions about "how much therapy do you do and how much does it help in the long run?" Those other parents gave me permission to not make myself crazy trying to do it all. I came out of the support session with new friends and renewed hope for the future.

- Because Liz's dad works for the federal government, she is entitled to health insurance for a "Child Incapable of Self Support." She doesn't have to be unemployed. Because her income falls below a certain guideline and she has a verified disability, she qualifies to be on his plan – Liz is covered for life. You really need to check into this program. Contact the HR office of the federal employee to find out what steps to take.

- This one is just for mothers. It is not your fault. I think in the back of our minds, many of us feel responsible for our child's problems. Maybe it was something we did when we were pregnant, maybe our child has a condition that is passed down only through the mother, maybe other people on our side of the family have similar conditions, or maybe we didn't ask enough questions. The fact of the matter is, any or all of these things may be true, but blaming yourself or God or Mother Nature or the universe doesn't change anything and doesn't help anybody. You may have these thoughts, but I urge you to let them go. Don't think about what you might have done, but what you can do and are doing.

- Depending on how long you have been a parent you have probably had people tell you they could never do what you are doing and that you are special and wonderful and a saint. My advice is to respond to these comments with a smile and a thank you. The people who say these things are sincerely sympathetic and they admire you. "We" know that we are just schlepping through each day doing the best we can for that day. On the other hand, there is no harm in taking credit for all you do either. So, as you read this, raise a glass of something to all the parents everywhere who are raising kids with disabilities and say, "Here's to Us. We're Terrific!"

Appendix B

Liziosities

A lot of Liz's behavior and social interactions can be chalked up to Pervasive Developmental Disorder or Autism or Hyperlexia or Intellectual Disability or any of the myriad of other labels that have been used to describe what is "wrong" with Liz. When all that is considered, there is still the Liz that I know, who is unique in all the world and who fits no one label. When I think of some of the things that make her so special, they are incidents or comments that don't fit neatly into any chapter of this book. So, rather than leave them on the cutting room floor, I have simply listed them, with the caveat that this list isn't the total Liz either. No list or collection of behaviors can accurately describe any person. This list is simply my reflection on the fascinating, funny, practical, take-no-prisoners woman who is my daughter.

❖   One Sunday when she was small, we took her to Mass much against her will. Bob always gave her a quarter to put in the collection plate. She stomped into the pew, turned to me and said, "And tell Dad not to give me a quarter, cause I ain't paying for this!"

❖ She came with us to a movie that I didn't realize was subtitled. She hated the movie and said angrily afterwards, "Don't ever take me to a movie with sign language again!"

❖ When my older brother, who had polio as a child, was in the hospital following a surgery completely unrelated to the polio, Liz sent him a Get Well Card. She added a personal note at the end that said, "I'm sorry you got polio, but I'm glad it's not contagious."

❖ For a long time, she related every moment in time to my younger brother's birthday. I started fifth grade ..... years after Denny's birthday. We went to the Cubs game .... years and .... days after the day Denny was born, and so on. We never knew why she did it, but it made Denny feel really important.

❖ She constantly makes me recognize how much we overthink things. She lost some weight recently and people kept asking her what her secret was. The question always elicited the same reply. "Figure out what's making you fat and quit eating it!"

❖ Her brother was trying to rationalize the fact that he had been dieting and working out and still weighed the same.

He said he was actually losing weight because muscle weighs more than fat. Liz, who missed her calling as a personal trainer, rolled her eyes and said, "If you weigh the same, you aren't losing weight."

❖ I showed her a photo of her niece and nephew that my daughter-in-law emailed me. "Aren't they darling?" I asked. Liz acknowledged that they were cute, but added, "I don't get as semi mental (sentimental) about the grandkids as you do."

❖ Ollie Webb died several years ago and Liz and I went to her funeral service. We walked up to the casket to say our last goodbye and, to my horror, Liz reached in and shook Ollie's arm. I whispered for her to stop and whisked her away hoping no one had noticed. When I asked her why she had done that, she shrugged and said, "Well, you never know."

❖ Life is without nuance for Liz. Her comments are unpolished. Sometimes they make me cringe, and sometimes they crack me up. Once I asked her to take drink orders from our guests. "The bald guy (of course said right in front of him) wants a beer."

❖ She is not a meddler. When I asked her what others were wearing to an event, she replied "I don't know. It's none of my business what other people wear."

❖ Her memory for some things is phenomenal. When her brothers had a paper route, one of them asked the other where a customer lived. Without looking up from "Wheel of Fortune," Lizzie rattled off the address. The boys began to throw out names to her and she was able to give them the house number of every customer. No one knows how or why she memorized them. I stopped updating my address\phone number book a long time ago. I just ask Liz for the current information.

❖ She used to know the license number of every car on our block. There are nineteen houses on our block and most people have two or even three cars. You do the math.

❖ An example of her literal interpretation of things: when a boy in junior high was giving Liz a hard time, I asked her what he looked like. Was he a black boy or a white boy? She replied, "Um, kind of gold."

❖ I love the way she sometimes turns a phrase. When I remarked that it had been a long time since I had eaten

168

French Silk Pie, she said it had been eight years. "Don't you remember? Your mother went to eternal rest in 2001 and we ate French Silk Pie on Dad's birthday the next week."

❖   Asked if she had three dollars to pay for something she wanted to buy, she answered no. She had four twenty dollar bills in her purse, but, indeed she did not have three dollars.

❖   Sometimes she knocks my socks off with something she knows. We were walking in the mountains one winter about five years ago. My friend and I and Liz were trying to navigate our way down a slippery slope. When we made it safely to level ground, my friend said, "Well, Liz, we came, we saw, we conquered." Liz said, "Don't give me that Julius Caesar stuff!"

❖   I've never been exactly clear about what Existentialism is, but I think Liz might have nailed it when we were visiting Martha's daughter and her triplets. Liz said to the little girl triplet, "So, Scout, did you ever think you would be a triplet?"

References

Kingsley, Emily Perl. "Welcome to Holland." c1987.

Pierce, Lauren. "The Butterfly," *IRCMS-Improving Reading Comprehension using Metacognitive Strategies-Third Grade Reading Passages.* NC State University. Web. May 2012.

Perske, R. "The Dignity of Risk and the Mentally Retarded" *Mental Retardation*, Vol.10, No. 1. February, 1972.

27500895R00099

Made in the USA
Lexington, KY
11 November 2013